£2·50

TREES FOR THE GARDEN

TREES FOR THE GARDEN

John Cushnie

Photography by Sarah Cuttle

KYLE CATHIE LIMITED

To Wilma

because of whom trees are only
the second great love of my life.

Love, John

First published in Great Britain in 2002 by
Kyle Cathie Limited
122 Arlington Road
London NW1 7HP
general.enquiries@kyle-cathie.com
www.kylecathie.com

ISBN 1 85626 445 9

© 2002 by John Cushnie
Photography © 2002 by Sarah Cuttle
See also other copyright acknowledgements on page 224

John Cushnie is hereby identified as the author of this work in
accordance with Section 77 of the Copyright, Designs and
Patents Act 1988.

A Cataloguing in Publication record for this title is available
from the British Library

Project editor Caroline Taggart
Design Mary Staples
Step-by-step photography Christopher Cormack
Illustrations Elizabeth Kay
Copy editor Sharon Amos
Production Lorraine Baird and Sha Huxtable

Page 1: *Malus* 'Dartmouth'
Page 2: *Prunus subhirtella* 'Flore-Pleno'
Page 3: Ash (*Fraxinus*) flowers opening before the leaves appear
This page: *Cercis siliquastrum*
Opposite: *Acer davidii*

Printed and bound in Singapore by Star Standard

CONTENTS

INTRODUCTION

WHO CAN SAY THAT THEY HAVE NEVER MARVELLED AT THE SIGHT OF AN ANCIENT TREE? Standing in the vicinity of an oak, giant redwood or pine that has survived for centuries is a sobering experience. If trees could talk, much of the detail of history would have to be rewritten.

In the past, trees have been worshipped and even today there are few people brave enough to cut down a 'fairy thorn' or bring a branch of may blossom indoors. It may be superstition, but the magical powers of trees are still cause for caution.

Wars have been won and lost on the availability of timber for ship building and charcoal making. The country's gain has been the country-side's loss, with whole forests disappearing under the axe. How different Scotland must have looked when pines clothed the landscape. Timber for house building and wood pulp for newsprint have further denuded our world of life-breathing trees.

Beloved by poets and essayists, it is small wonder that trees have gained an aesthetic value in the garden. Asian gardeners have, for a thousand years, offered trees a home where their beauty could be better appreciated. In the western world today, trees have never been more fashionable. We understand that they form part of the equation for our continued existence on the planet. Some years ago, an American tree producer coined the slogan 'We grow clean air machines'. He deserved to sell lots of plants.

With the help of government grants, trees are once again starting to cover our bare hillsides. Public authorities are planting up open spaces, while gardeners are anxious to buy the newest variety on the market. It is

a move in the right direction and one to be applauded, but only if we take heed of thousands of years of tree knowledge. The slogan for today should be 'The right tree in the right place'. In this book, I will attempt to help you choose the right tree for your particular place – and be assured, there is a suitable ornamental tree for all but the smallest of gardens.

Every garden should have at least one tree and it is a boring and uninspiring landscape that is devoid of their shape and structure. Trees are invaluable in garden design, providing a vertical aspect and guaranteeing a three-dimensional look to the smallest of plots.

In the eighteenth century, Alexander Pope said that 'all gardening is landscape painting' and in garden design we are painting a picture. Like any good artist we must keep the centre open with no clutter to shorten the view. Similarly, the show-garden style of design, where the plot is packed with plants to give an impression of maturity, is to be avoided. Trees need space to grow without being overcrowded. Specimens – single plants set away from any others – may be used to draw the eye to the side or far end of the garden.

Any artist would be envious of the range of colours available for use in the garden. We are spoilt with an embarrassment of riches of leaf colour –

Trees with an eye-catching bark like this common beech (*Fagus sylvatica*) provide interest all year round. Pruning beech to make a hedge keeps them to a manageable size and the trees will then retain their attractive crinkly dead leaves throughout the winter.

red, orange, purple, yellow and the 40 shades of green, many of which are transformed in autumn to every imaginable tint. The flowers of magnolia, cornus and cherry and the fruit of crab apple and rowan add variety to the palette, while the colour and texture of the bark of acer, birch and cherry ensure interest on the dullest winter day. Movement to catch the eye is provided by the fluttering of the leaves of poplars and whitebeam, showing their downy white reverse. If positioned correctly a tree can also provide cool shade from the sun or shelter from biting cold winds.

A selection of trees chosen with attention to detail can put on a continuous display with spectacular shows of leaf, bark, flower and berry. The performances will overlap and some trees may be outclassed by their neighbours. Leaf colour, such as that of *Robinia* 'Frisia', may be relied on to

LEFT Spring glory *par excellence* – this magnolia underplanted with daffodils will fill your garden with cheer a month or two before many other plants reach their peak.

RIGHT Most people plant ornamental cherries for their glorious spring blossom, and you will see plenty of examples of that in the course of this book. But with some, when the blooms have gone and the leaves have fallen, there is still the richness of the bark to enjoy.

LEFT *Amelanchier lamarckii* – one of my favourite trees – can compete with the best of them for spring blossom, but is also worth growing for the berries that follow, and for its autumn colour.

ABOVE Trees of the *Sorbus* genus (rowans) are among the best for autumn berries. *S. esserteauana* (above left) has the familiar profusion of red berries, while the variety 'Joseph Rock' (above right) surprises with a delicate shade of creamy-yellow.

take over from fading flowers of another species that needs time to metamorphose before returning to centre stage as fruit or berries. In the dead of winter, the bark of birch and willow stands out among the bare twigs. My personal favourite, the snowy mespilus (*Amelanchier* 'Ballerina') will, on its own, provide interest for eight months of the year with blossom, berries and autumn leaf colour.

Occasionally a tree really surprises us. We tend to think of rowan trees, for example, as having red or orange-red fruit, but some varieties have a mind of their own. *Sorbus* 'Joseph Rock' has white flowers in spring with superb autumn leaf colour in shades of orange, copper, red and purple. The large clusters of fruits are creamy-yellow, deepening to honey yellow by early winter.

The handkerchief tree (*Davidia involucrata*) is not striking in leaf, but a mature tree in late spring is an astounding sight. It covers itself in flowers, each with two large pure white bracts, giving rise to its popular name. It is also sometimes referred to as the ghost tree or dove tree.

What tree to plant

There are small trees and there are large trees. The problem for the gardener is that some so-called small trees eventually become much larger than envisaged. In a small garden they may dominate to the extent that they have to be removed. The problem may be caused by impulse buying, incorrect labelling or bad advice from the seller. Plant labels tend to suggest a tree's height after 10 years; where they do give the ultimate size, it may well be understated to make the tree seem more suitable for smaller gardens. By the time you realise your tree has outgrown its allotted space, the garden-centre guarantee has long since expired and the original advice has been forgotten. Even if the information on the ultimate height of the tree is accurate, the spread of the branches may not get a mention. This may result in damage to property or branches overhanging the road in a dangerous way.

Throughout these pages I will endeavour to be honest regarding the size, shape and speed of growth of garden trees. It is in everyone's interest to leave behind us trees that will continue to give pleasure to future generations, without becoming a nuisance.

Before deciding on a species or variety of tree, you might ask yourself the following questions.

◆ Do you want a deciduous tree (one that loses its leaves in winter) or would you prefer an evergreen species where the foliage is on display all year?

◆ What purpose will the plant serve? Will it be ornamental, with flower, fruit, leaf colour or decorative bark playing an important role? Is it to be a specimen on the lawn where shape is important? Or do you need a tough screening copse for privacy and to filter the wind?

◆ Trees are essential providers of shelter and food for wildlife. Is that an important consideration for you?

◆ How many trees have you space for and how many do you want?

◆ What are your soil and climatic conditions like? Do you know what will grow there?

There is an enormous variety of crab apples to choose from, but all produce spectacular spring blossom, followed by attractive fruits, some of which are edible.

Chamaecyparis obtusa 'Nana Aurea' – an enormous name for a genuinely 'dwarf' tree. It is ideal for rock gardens and other small spaces, as it will never reach a height of greater than 2m (6ft 6in).

All these questions bar the last one come down to personal choice but, where garden space is limited, may cause heated discussion. However, when the dust settles, it is the soil type and climate that may well decide the variety for you. For information about specific sites and situations see the section *Six of the Best*, which begins on page 18, and for the requirements of individual trees, see the *Directory*, which begins on page 114.

The shape of things to come

Landscape designers like trees because of their outline and habit of growth. Unlike shrubs, they are usually consistent in shape, allowing the designer to predict accurately the way the tree will look in 20 or 50 years' time. There are a number of shapes to choose from.

◆ **Columnar or fastigiate varieties** grow into narrow upright trees with ascending branches; for example, the pale pink flowering cherry (*Prunus* 'Amanogawa'). Its stiff branches refuse to sway in a spring breeze, allowing the blossom to adorn the tree rather than becoming confetti on the ground.

◆ **Weeping trees** are those whose branches bend straight down. None does it better than the silver-leaved weeping pear, although the weeping birch is elegantly pendulous with drooping branches and an airy grace.

◆ **A rounded or domed-headed tree** tends to spread its branches and, in time, make a large specimen, needing a lot of growing space for the canopy. The traditional English elm, so wonderfully depicted in Constable's paintings, forms a narrow-domed head. Wych elm, chestnut, oak and beech will, in maturity, make large broad-domed specimens.

Trees with a special shape, such as a weeping or fastigiate habit, need a prominent place in the garden to show themselves off.

Buying a tree

If there is a nursery in your area that grows trees, that is the best place to try. The staff will know about trees, their likes and dislikes, and will have pride in what they sell. A friendly garden centre, where staff are prepared to take the time to help with your choice, is the next best option. Further down the list come street markets and supermarkets.

Other conditions being equal, the tree most likely to succeed is one that has been lifted and transplanted in the nursery each winter, allowing it to build up a fibrous root system. When offered for sale, it will be lifted with a rootball without the soil falling off. Such plants are available only from late autumn until the buds swell in early spring. Conifers may be lifted from

BELOW A classic example of a fastigiate or upright habit – the golden Irish yew *Taxus baccata* 'Fastigiata Aureomarginata'.

LEFT What could be more different from the disciplined form of the yew opposite than this weeping pear (*Pyrus salicifolia pendula*)? It droops elegantly in this romantic corner.

BELOW Another example of the weeping habit – this is *Morus alba pendula.* Slow growing and late to come into leaf, but worth the wait.

mid-autumn to mid-spring, providing the soil is moist. Try to arrange to be at the nursery when your trees are being dug out of the ground. You will be able to check the roots for damage.

Container-grown trees may be planted at any time of year. When the container is removed, the sign of a well-grown tree is that the roots should hold the soil in place. During the growing season, avoid containerised trees that have been potted only recently. The soil will fall off when the container is removed, leaving the roots bare and causing a check to the tree's growth. If it is in leaf it may die. A good test is to lift the tree by the stem. If the roots appear to be pulling out of the compost, don't buy it. New stock of container-grown trees is usually delivered to garden centres in late autumn and by spring the best plants will have been sold.

Root-balled trees – large trees lifted with the soil attached to the roots and wrapped in wire mesh and hessian – are similar to container-grown.

Avoid ball-wrapped plants, where bare-root trees are put through a machine which packs peat or compost round the roots and wraps it in hessian. The compost often works loose, hanging in the wrapping below the roots and resulting in a high death rate.

Bare-rooted, deciduous trees are dug up for sale after leaf fall and, if planted before the new year, they have a better chance of becoming established before growth starts in spring.

Trees with a single, straight stem or trunk are referred to as standards. A half standard has 1-1.2m (3-4ft) of clear stem before the branches appear. With full standards the branches are allowed to form at 1.8m (6ft). Commercially they are graded by the circumference of the stem at 1m (3ft) above soil level. A girth of 6-8cm (2½-3½in) is the smallest size for most standard cherry, rowan or crab apple trees, for example.

Trees are also sold as 'whips' – two-year-old trees that are usually offered as bare-root plants.

Most tree nurseries sell anything from one-year seedlings 30cm (12in) high to extra heavy standard trees 5-7m (16-23ft) high. Specialist growers

ABOVE Different again – *Acer griseum* branching less than 1m (3ft) above the ground, giving a much fuller, more rounded shape.

LEFT *Prunus* x *subhirtella* 'Autumnalis Rosea', a winter-flowering cherry, is in bloom for four months at the darkest time of the year. This means there is a good chance you could buy a fairly large container-grown tree in flower.

with sophisticated lifting equipment and transport can even supply mature specimen trees that are 15m (50ft) plus.

Landscape designers have made multi-stemmed birch trees fashionable. The young tree is cut back in the nursery, causing it to produce side shoots from the base, resulting in the tree having a minimum of three trunks. In your own garden, planting a clump of three whips angled outwards will achieve the desired effect more quickly and cheaply.

When is a tree not a tree?

Deciding whether a plant is a tree or a shrub can be confusing. So when is a tree not a tree? The wrong answer is: when it is not very big. There are trees that, when mature, are miniature in size. Some varieties of Japanese maple, for example, grow to only 3m (10ft). Yet they are every bit as much a tree as a sycamore, which will quickly reach 30m (100ft).

The broad definition of a tree is a long-lived woody perennial, which may be deciduous or evergreen. It often has a single stem, although there are exceptions: a multi-stemmed silver birch is certainly classed as a tree. Further confusion arises from the fact that the banana plant is always referred to as a tree but is really a herbaceous perennial, while *Cotoneaster* 'Cornubia' and *Magnolia wilsonii* can be described as either large shrubs or small trees.

I tend to be relaxed about the whole thing, being prepared to call an enormous shrub a tree, as in the case of a specimen of *Griselinia littoralis* near my home which is 12m (40ft) high. Hence in this book you will find entries for Mount Etna broom (*Genista aetnensis*), *Cotoneaster* 'Cornubia' and *Rhododendron macabeanum*, although there is a case for calling all of these shrubs. You'll also find ground-covering conifers: these qualify as trees, even though some may never grow higher than 75cm (30in).

SIX OF THE BEST

The marvellous thing about gardens is that no two are the same. They may differ in size and shape, but it is their cultural differences which make gardening such a fascinating lifetime's work. Ground may vary from light, well-drained, impoverished soil to heavy, sticky, wet, cold clay. The site may benefit from full sun or be shaded for most of the day. An exposed garden will have different requirements to a sheltered situation.

There are trees which will thrive in what, at first, seems to be an inhospitable site. The tree's long-term success will depend upon your choosing a species that can cope with the particular conditions of your garden.

In this section of 'trees for special purposes', you will find five tried and tested trees for every situation. There is also a sixth suggestion of a species that is a little bit out of the ordinary, just to impress your neighbours.

Full details of all the trees included here can be found in the Directory which starts on page 114.

LEFT *Stewartii pseudocamellia* is spectacular in flower, autumn leaf and bark, but to perform well it needs a sheltered site and acid soil.

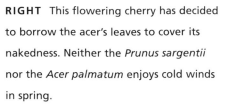

RIGHT This flowering cherry has decided to borrow the acer's leaves to cover its nakedness. Neither the *Prunus sargentii* nor the *Acer palmatum* enjoys cold winds in spring.

Trees for clay soils

Some clay soils that are wet in winter become dry, hard and cracked in summer. Other sites only appear to be wet because the soil surface has been compacted, preventing the water from soaking down through the soil. Breaking the surface crust may solve this problem. Only a proper drainage system will offer a cure for soils that are truly wet or waterlogged all year, although an alternative is to raise the soil above the water table in a mound, allowing the tree to spread its roots above the waterlogged area. Where this isn't an option you will have to plant trees listed below, which are tolerant of cold, wet, winter soil conditions.

Betula nigra

Sorbus aucuparia

Amelanchier 'Ballerina'
SNOWY MESPILUS

Deciduous
Height 6m [20ft]
Spread 7m [23ft]
◆ Tolerates partial shade but dislikes an alkaline soil
◆ This is my favourite small tree, providing interest for most of the year with leaf colour, flowers and fruit

Betula nigra
RIVER BIRCH, BLACK BIRCH

Deciduous
Height 18m [60ft]
Spread 12m [40ft]
◆ Tolerates exposed sites
◆ Dislikes a shallow alkaline soil
◆ In autumn, the long, dark green leaves quickly turn to deep yellow, contrasting with the rich brown bark

Rhamnus cathartica
COMMON BUCKTHORN

Deciduous
Height 6m [20ft]
Spread 5m [16ft]
◆ Dislikes deep shade
◆ Clusters of bright red fruit contrast with the golden autumnal foliage
  Unfortunately, birds often eat the display

one to impress the neighbours

Magnolia 'Wada's Memory'

Salix babylonica
var. pekinensis 'Tortuosa'
CORKSCREW WILLOW

Deciduous
Height 15m [50ft]
Spread 8m [26ft]
◆ Likes a sunny site
◆ Prune young plants hard to encourage
new growth
◆ Dislikes shallow alkaline soil
◆ The young growths, with their manic
twists, are loved by flower arrangers

Sorbus aucuparia
ROWAN, MOUNTAIN ASH

Deciduous
Height 15m [50ft]
Spread 7m [23ft]
◆ Likes a sunny site
◆ Dislikes an alkaline soil
◆ The large bunches of orange-red berries
may be made into a deep orange-coloured,
slightly bitter jelly, ideal with pheasant

Magnolia 'Wada's Memory'
SWEET BAY

Deciduous
Height 9m [30ft]
Spread 7m [23ft]
◆ Likes a humus-rich soil with a
surface mulch
◆ Dislikes an alkaline soil
◆ Masses of white, sweetly scented flowers
appear in late spring, when they are prone
to damage from late frosts

Trees for acid soil

Soils that are dark brown in colour and rich in organic material, such as those found in peat bogs and woodland, are usually acidic. An acid or ericaceous soil has its fans: birch and sorbus love it while rhododendrons won't grow on anything else. Clay soils can also be acid, but may need to be drained or opened up by adding grit before trees can be planted.

Ilex aquifolium 'Ferox Argentea'

Eucryphia glutinosa

Betula pendula
SILVER BIRCH

Deciduous
Height 25m [80ft]
Spread 10m [33ft]
◆ Prefers sun or light shade
◆ Dislikes being transplanted as a large plant
◆ Without fail, this tree will produce soft yellow autumn leaf colour to brighten the dullest day

Eucryphia glutinosa

Semi evergreen or deciduous
Height 10m [33ft]
Spread 5m [16ft]
◆ Tolerates cold winds
◆ Prefers the surface of the soil to be shaded
◆ In mid to late summer this tree buries itself in fragrant white flowers

Ilex aquifolium 'Ferox Argentea'
VARIEGATED HEDGEHOG HOLLY

Evergreen
Height 8m [26ft]
Spread 4m [13ft]
◆ Needs full sun
◆ Dislikes heavy, wet soil
◆ Grown for its striking spiny green leaves edged with creamy-white margins

one to impress the neighbours

Ailanthus altissima

Populus tremula 'Pendula'
WEEPING ASPEN

Deciduous
Height and spread 7m [23ft]

◆ Enjoys a moist, well-fertilized soil
◆ Dislikes growing in shade
◆ Even on a calm day the leaves shiver and shake, bronze in spring, then green turning yellow in autumn

Robinia pseudoacacia 'Frisia'
FALSE ACACIA, LOCUST TREE

Deciduous
Height 14m [46ft]
Spread 6m [20ft]

◆ Needs shelter from strong winds
◆ Prone to sucker at the base
◆ The foliage is kept busy – butter-yellow in spring, green-yellow in summer, turning orange before leaf drop

Ailanthus altissima
TREE OF HEAVEN

Deciduous
Height 25m [80ft]
Spread 15m [50ft]

◆ Easily grown from seed
◆ Prone to sucker at the base
◆ Panicles of green female flowers produce winged seed which colour to a brilliant red in late summer

Trees for alkaline soil

Soils with a pH above 7 are alkaline or limy [you can buy an easy-to-use tester kit from the garden centre]. Where the site overlies chalk, the topsoil tends to dry out in summer restricting the choice of suitable trees. Alkaline soil is usually well drained and will warm up quickly in spring. Digging in lots of compost or farmyard manure whenever you plant will help to retain moisture and, over time, will also increase the depth of soil.

Koelreuteria paniculata

Crataegus laciniata

Cercis siliquastrum
JUDAS TREE

Deciduous
Height and spread 10m [33ft]
- Likes a deep, loam soil
- Dislikes transplanting
- Beautiful purple seed pods follow the show of purple-pink flowers in late spring

Crataegus laciniata
CUT-LEAF HAWTHORN

Deciduous
Height 6m [20ft], spread 5m [16ft]
- May be grown as a hedge
- Dislikes waterlogged soil
- Deeply lobed dark green leaves, fewer thorns than other species and large orange-red fruit make this a choice thorn for the garden

Koelreuteria paniculata
GOLDEN RAIN TREE, PRIDE OF INDIA

Deciduous
Height 10m [33ft]
Spread 9m [30ft]
- Prefers a site in full sun
- Dislikes waterlogged soil
- The large panicles of bright yellow flowers appear in late summer when most trees are relying on leaf or berry for colour

one to impress the neighbours

Albizia julibrissin f. *rosea*

Laburnum alpinum
SCOTCH LABURNUM

Deciduous

Height and spread 7m [23ft]

◆ Likes a sunny site

◆ Bright yellow trailing racemes of flowers are produced in early summer and exude a delicious fragrance

Malus floribunda
JAPANESE CRAB APPLE

Deciduous

Height and spread 10m [33ft]

◆ Dislikes late frosts at flowering time

◆ This crab covers itself in flowers. The buds are red, the open flowers pink on the outside and white on the inside. A spectacle in spring.

Albizia julibrissin f. rosea
SILK TREE

Deciduous

Height 6m [20ft]

Spread 4m [13ft]

◆ Needs a sheltered site in full sun

◆ Unfortunately, in America, this tree suffers from fusarium disease

◆ In summer, clusters of fluffy pink flowers stand out from the mid-green ferny foliage, followed by long seed pods

Trees for dry & sunny sites

Gleditsia triacanthos 'Sunburst'

Most trees, by their nature, grow well in shade. There are, however, some trees that tolerate full sun and these are particularly useful when designing for small sunny gardens. You need to be aware that gravelly soils, without humus, are free draining and, when coupled with a summer drought, may cause young trees to become stressed.

There is a difference between a free-draining dry soil in a warm, wet climate such as Great Britain and a sun-baked. frost-free Southern European or South African soil. During a cold, damp British winter, the temperature need drop by only 1-2 degrees Celsius [2-4 Fahrenheit] to kill plants. Half-hardy and frost-tender trees will only survive until the first 'below average' winter. Where the atmosphere and the soil are dry, frosty conditions are less severe on plants. For example, my own garden in Northern Ireland is adequately watered with approximately 800mm [32in] of rain each year. Yet the top 15cm [6in] frequently dries out to the point where I resort to watering young plants that haven't had chance to establish. This is not the result of a hot, dry season but a lack of moisture-retentive humus in a gravelly soil, deposited before my time by a glacier. However, once trees become established they will send out roots in search of water.

Genista aetnensis

Celtis occidentalis

NETTLE TREE OR HACKBERRY

Deciduous
Height 20m [66ft]
Spread 13m [43ft]
- Needs a warm site in full sun
- Dislikes wet conditions
- After a warm summer, the tree covers itself in edible red, purple or yellow fruit

Genista aetnensis

MOUNT ETNA BROOM

Deciduous
Height and spread 8m [26ft]
- Enjoys an impoverished soil
- Dislikes hard pruning
- The wild plants growing on the slopes of Mount Etna make an astonishing display of gold in summer

Gleditsia triacanthos 'Sunburst'

HONEY LOCUST

Deciduous
Height and spread 10m [33ft]
- Plant in full sun
- Dislikes spring frosts
- Grown for its foliage, the display starts gold in spring, turning to green-yellow in summer and finally a soft butter-yellow in autumn

one to impress the neighbours

Acacia rhetinodes

Maackia amurensis

Deciduous
Height 15m [50ft]
Spread 9m [30ft]
◆ Likes a rich soil
◆ Dislikes alkaline soil
◆ Although slow-growing, it flowers early in
life. The white flowers appear in profusion
in mid to late summer.

Sophora japonica
JAPANESE PAGODA TREE

Deciduous
Height 30m [100ft]
Spread 15m [50ft]
◆ Needs full sun
◆ Dislikes cold winds
◆ Long, creamy-white, fragrant panicles in
late summer are followed by trailing seed
pods that resemble a string of beads

Acacia rhetinodes
SILVER WATTLE

Evergreen
Height 6m [20ft]
Spread 4m [13ft]
◆ Prefers an acid soil in a sheltered situation
◆ Dislikes hard pruning
◆ The clusters of lemon-yellow flowers
usually open in summer, but may appear
from late spring to autumn

Trees for coastal sites

There are disadvantages to maritime sites: wind-blown salt can be deposited on the leaves, while cold easterly winds tend to burn the foliage of evergreen trees. On the positive side, light, free-draining soils can be an advantage and frost is seldom a problem close to the shore. The trees listed below can cope with coastal sites. And if you plant a windbreak of these tough, salt-tolerant trees as a first line of defence, other less-resistant species can be grown in the shelter provided.

Crataegus x *lavallei* 'Carrierei'

Hippophae rhamnoides

Crataegus x lavallei 'Carrierei'
HAWTHORN

Semi-evergreen
Height 7m [23ft]
Spread 8m [26ft]
◆ Dislikes waterlogged soil
◆ After a dry summer the dark green leaves turn red in autumn before falling, leaving the orange-red berries to hang on into winter

Hippophae rhamnoides
SEA BUCKTHORN

Deciduous
Height and spread 6m [20ft]
◆ Prefers an alkaline, well-drained soil
◆ In early autumn female plants produce masses of orange-red berries which often remain on the branches for most of the winter

Populus alba
WHITE POPLAR

Deciduous
Height 30m [100ft]
Spread 15m [50ft]
◆ Succeeds in most soils, even dry conditions
◆ Dark green leaves which are silvery-white on the underside turn yellow in autumn in Britain, while in North America they become red

one to impress the neighbours

Arbutus unedo

Sorbus aria 'Lutescens'
WHITEBEAM

Deciduous
Height 10m [33ft]
Spread 7m [23ft]
◆ Succeeds in acid or alkaline soil
◆ Autumn leaf colour is great, but is easily surpassed by the large clusters of bright scarlet berries

Tamarix ramosissima 'Pink Cascade'
TAMARISK

Deciduous
Height and spread 5m [16ft]
◆ Needs a light soil in full sun
◆ Dislikes draughty sites
◆ A deceptively delicate-looking plant with feathery foliage and plumes of pink flowers

Arbutus unedo
STRAWBERRY TREE

Evergreen
Height and spread 7m [23ft]
◆ Likes a well-drained site in full sun, sheltered from cold winds
◆ Tolerates an alkaline soil
◆ The 'strawberry' fruit ripen to red at the same time as the white, pink-tinged autumn flowers open. The bark is stunning, too.

Trees for windy sites

Biting, cold winds cause havoc to unprotected plants. The roots of trees can be loosened or even blown out of the ground. Trees themselves are the best form of protection, filtering the wind rather than stopping it. A solid obstacle, such as a wall, pushes the wind over the top where it forms turbulence inside, at a distance of three to four times the height of the wall. Instead, a deep shelterbelt of close-planted trees, deciduous or evergreen, will slow the force of wind.

Laburnum x *watereri* 'Vossii'

Crataegus laevigata 'Paul's Scarlet'

Alnus cordata
ITALIAN ALDER

Deciduous
Height 25m [80ft]
Spread 7m [23ft]
◆ Will tolerate dry soil
◆ Dislikes full shade
◆ Bright, glossy green foliage and green cones which turn black in autumn make this an attractive garden tree

Crataegus laevigata 'Paul's Scarlet'
PINK MAY

Deciduous
Height and spread 8m [26ft]
◆ Makes a good hedge
◆ Dislikes a waterlogged site
◆ In late spring this tree is laden with clusters of small, dark pink, double flowers

Fagus sylvatica
COMMON BEECH

Deciduous
Height 25m [80ft]
Spread 15m [50ft]
◆ Will grow on chalk soils
◆ Dislikes waterlogged conditions
◆ As a hedge it holds its russet-brown autumn leaf colouring throughout the winter

one to impress the neighbours

Fraxinus excelsior 'Jaspidea'

Laburnum x watereri 'Vossii'
GOLDEN RAIN

Deciduous

Height and spread 9m [30ft]

◆ Prefers a well-drained soil in a sunny situation

◆ Grown to form an arch, the trailing racemes of golden flowers are a treat to walk under in early summer

Sorbus intermedia 'Brouwers'
SWEDISH WHITEBEAM

Deciduous

Height 8m [26ft]

Spread 5m [16ft]

◆ Likes a rich, well-drained soil

◆ Dislikes alkaline soil

◆ Eye-catching with its glossy, dark green leaves which are grey on the underside, and bright red berries in autumn

Fraxinus excelsior 'Jaspidea'
GOLDEN ASH

Deciduous

Height 20m [66ft]

Spread 12m [40ft]

◆ Prefers a sunny situation

◆ Dislikes alkaline soil

◆ Young stems are bright yellow, showing off the jet black winter buds

Trees to grow against walls

In this situation the choice of tree is critical. Most trees are too vigorous. Even small trees produce an extensive root system which will, in time, damage old walls where the foundation is weak. The soil at the base of a wall may need to be improved if there is lots of builder's debris and lime residue from mortar. The eaves of the building may prevent rain reaching the soil, causing drought conditions. Pruning will be necessary to prevent stems obscuring windows and blocking doors.

Walls warmed by the sun are best suited for trees that are tender and needing shelter, like those listed here. Avoid planting spring-flowering trees such as camellias, apple, plums and peaches against walls that enjoy the morning sun: a late spring frost followed by the rays of the early morning sun will destroy the flowers. North-facing walls [south-facing in the southern hemisphere] are cold and shaded, but may be planted with tough trees such as the Portuguese laurel [*Prunus lusitanica*].

Acacia dealbata

Olea europaea

Acacia dealbata
MIMOSA, SILVER WATTLE

Evergreen
Height 15m [50ft]
Spread 5m [16ft]
◆ Needs a sheltered site in full sun
◆ Dislikes an alkaline soil
◆ Known in Britain as the 'florists' mimosa', the buttercup-yellow flowers appear in winter and spring

Azara microphylla 'Variegata'

Evergreen
Height 8m [26ft]
Spread 4m [13ft]
◆ Will grow in shade
◆ Dislikes cold winds
◆ A charming tree with tiny green and cream variegated leaves and vanilla-scented winter flowers

Magnolia grandiflora 'Little Gem'
BULL BAY

Evergreen
Height 6m [20ft]
Spread 3m [10ft]
◆ Will tolerate dry, alkaline soil
◆ Dislikes cold winds
◆ Flowering in summer and early autumn, the creamy-white flowers exude a wonderful perfume

one to impress the neighbours

Osmanthus yunnanensis

Olea europaea

OLIVE

Evergreen

Height and spread 9m [30ft]

- Needs a well-drained soil in full sun
- Dislikes cold, wet summers
- If you grow one of these in a temperate climate, you may never see an olive or the creamy-white fragrant flowers, but it is still worth planting for the foliage

Sophora tetraptera

KOWHAI

Evergreen

Height 10m [33ft]

Spread 4m [13ft]

- Loves a warm sunny wall
- Dislikes transplanting
- Deep golden-yellow spring flowers are followed by unusual winged seed pods

Osmanthus yunnanensis

Evergreen

Height and spread 9m [30ft]

- Tolerates hard pruning
- Dislikes cold, wet soil in winter
- Highly fragrant creamy-white flowers appear in late winter, followed by purple fruit covered with a white bloom

Trees for small gardens

The size of your garden will, more than any other factor, stipulate which tree is suitable. A small tree in a large garden may look out of place but a large tree in too small a space will suffer and eventually destroy all the neighbouring plants. Trees cast shade and planted in the wrong place may block light and sun from your neighbour.

Yet small gardens deserve a suitably sized tree to act as a feature. The smallest of trees will attract wildlife and add shape, colour and year-round interest to a garden.

You may decide that filling the available space with a tree will mean sacrificing too many other plants. An alternative is to plant trees in containers and, when they become an embarrassment, pass them on to a good – larger – home.

Prunus 'Amanogawa'

Caragana aborescens 'Pendula'
WEEPING PEA TREE

Deciduous
Height 2m [6ft 6in]
Spread 1.5m [5ft]
◆ Needs full sun
◆ Dislikes wet soil
◆ Flowering in late spring, the clusters of yellow flowers are followed by long, thin, brown seed pods

Cotoneaster 'Hybridus Pendulus'
WEEPING COTONEASTER

Evergreen or semi-evergreen
Height and spread 2m [6ft 6in] if grown as a standard
◆ Prefers a well-drained soil
◆ Needs to be staked
◆ Clusters of bright red berries cover the tree in autumn, providing a quick snack for every bird for miles

Malus 'Royal Beauty'
CRAB APPLE

Deciduous
Height and spread 2m [6ft 6in]
◆ Prefers a position in full sun
◆ Dislikes waterlogged soil
◆ Dark red-purple flowers in spring give way to deep red fruit. The young leaves are deep red, turning green

one to impress the neighbours

Salix caprea 'Kilmarnock'

Acer palmatum 'Shindeshojo'

Prunus 'Amanogawa'
FLOWERING CHERRY

Deciduous
Height 7m [23ft]
Spread 3m [10ft]
◆ Likes full sun
◆ Dislikes wet soil
◆ In spring the pale pink, fragrant flowers
  are held on stiff branches, making them
  less prone to wind damage

Salix caprea 'Kilmarnock'
KILMARNOCK WILLOW

Deciduous
Height and spread 2m [6ft 6in]
◆ Prefers a sunny site
◆ Dislikes an alkaline soil
◆ The silvery catkins appear in winter,
  opening to display their golden anthers

Acer palmatum 'Shindeshojo'
JAPANESE MAPLE

Deciduous
Height and spread 2m [6ft 6in]
◆ Likes a soil rich in leaf mould
◆ Dislikes cold winds in spring
◆ The new foliage is red, turning to pink
  mixed with creamy-white and green.
  By early autumn it is orange-red.

Trees for average gardens

It is difficult to be specific about the size of the average garden but, with the increasing cost of land for building, new gardens tend to be smaller rather than larger. A rear garden 13-15m [43-50ft] wide and 20-25m [66-80ft] long will, in years to come, be considered bigger than average.

Always take your neighbours into account when planting a tree that will make a sizable plant. Blocking daylight, obstructing a view or problems with tree roots are just some of the ways trees can cause annoyance.

A useful trick is to design into your landscape an interesting tree at the furthest boundary from the house. By drawing your eye to that point, the garden will appear to be larger. Space in the average-sized garden will permit more than one tree. There might be room for a specimen flowering cherry, a birch with interesting bark and perhaps a fruiting crab apple or a rowan tree showing off its autumn colour.

Malus 'Golden Hornet'

Paulownia tomentosa

Betula utilis var. jacquemontii
HIMALAYAN BIRCH

   Deciduous
   Height 18m [60ft]
   Spread 10m [33ft]
   ◆ Will grow in full sun or partial shade
   ◆ Dislikes waterlogged soil
   ◆ The bark is so smooth you feel like giving it a pat with your hand

Malus 'Golden Hornet'
CRAB APPLE

   Deciduous
   Height 10m [33ft]
   Spread 7m [23ft]
   ◆ Likes a well-drained soil
   ◆ Dislikes deep shade
   ◆ In late spring the pink flower buds open to white and are followed, in autumn, by golden yellow crab apples

Paulownia tomentosa
FOXGLOVE TREE, EMPRESS TREE

   Deciduous
   Height 11m [36ft]
   Spread 8m [26ft]
   ◆ Enjoys full sun
   ◆ Dislikes cold winds in spring
   ◆ The flower buds form in autumn, opening in spring as foxglove-shaped lilac-purple spikes of bloom with a violet fragrance

one to impress the neighbours

Laburnocytisus 'Adamii'

Prunus 'Spire'
FLOWERING CHERRY

Deciduous
Height 10m [33ft]
Spread 6m [20ft]
◆ Prefers a site in full sun
◆ Prune in summer if necessary
◆ The new leaves open bronze, change to deep green and finally turn to glorious shades of orange, yellow and red. Soft pink flowers appear in spring.

Sorbus commixta
MOUNTAIN ASH

Deciduous
Height 10m [33ft]
Spread 6m [20ft]
◆ Likes an acid, well-manured site
◆ For weeks the orange-red berries are almost hidden by the autumn leaves, which change from red to scarlet and finally to crimson

Laburnocytisus 'Adamii'
ADAM'S LABURNUM

Deciduous
Height 8m [26ft]
Spread 5m 16[t]
◆ Dislikes waterlogged soil
◆ Remove any suckers that appear at ground level
◆ A real 'dolly mixture' of flowers: yellow, purple and coppery pink

Trees for large gardens

One way of landscaping on a large scale is to divide the garden into compartments such as kitchen garden, water feature, ornamental, secret and cottage sections. Trees become the backbone of the large garden whether as specimens on the lawn, planted to add height to shrub beds or perhaps to form an avenue. They may be used to frame a distant view or, where necessary, to obscure an eyesore such as a factory, outbuilding or electricity pylon.

Liquidambar styraciflua

Aesculus x *carnea* 'Briotii'

Acer platanoides 'Crimson Sentry'
RED-LEAVED NORWAY MAPLE

Deciduous
Height 11m [36ft]
Spread 5m [16ft]
◆ Will grow in most soils
◆ Dislikes heavy, wet conditions
◆ A striking tree with red-purple leaves from spring until late autumn

Aesculus x carnea 'Briotii'
RED HORSE CHESTNUT

Deciduous
Height 18m [60ft]
Spread 13m [42ft]
◆ Suits most soils
◆ Position it where the large leaves won't cause a problem in autumn
◆ Upright 'candles' of dark red flowers, each with a yellow centre, appear in early summer

Fagus sylvatica 'Dawyck Purple'
FASTIGIATE PURPLE BEECH

Deciduous
Height 20m [66ft]
Spread 4m [13ft]
◆ Leaf colour best in full sun
◆ Dislikes being transplanted when large
◆ The leaves are a deep purple, each with a wavy edge

one to impress the neighbours

Rhododendron macabeanum

Liquidambar styraciflua
SWEET GUM

Deciduous
Height 20m [66ft]
Spread 10m [33ft]
- Prefers a well-drained, acid soil
- Needs full sun for good autumn leaf colour
- Grown for its brilliant autumn foliage in yellow, orange, red and maroon

Malus 'Neville Copeman'
CRAB APPLE

Deciduous
Height and spread 9m [30ft]
- Likes a well-drained soil in full sun
- Dislikes late spring frosts
- Dark wine-red apple blossom is followed by orange-red fruit

Rhododendron macabeanum

Evergreen
Height 15m [50ft]
Spread 5m [16ft]
- Needs an acid soil
- Dislikes cold spring winds
- The large leaves are dark green and grey-white on the underside; pale yellow flowers blotched with purple appear in early spring

Trees for spring display

There is something about spring and all it promises. Bare branches seem unwilling to camouflage themselves, then suddenly they are fully clothed. Their leafy outfits put fashion designers to shame. While their individual style remains constant it is received with enthusiasm each year.

Trees that flower in spring need protection from the worst of the elements. Biting cold winds and late frosts may wipe out a spring display before it happens. Spring may be a short season, crowded out by a late winter and an early, dry summer. Other years, we are blessed with an early, mild spring when the new foliage bursts out of fat buds and keeps its freshness until the leaves mature.

Spring is often a dry period with little rain until early summer. Recently planted trees will suffer if the roots are deprived of moisture. Water them well, making sure the whole of the root area is wet, and then cover the base of the tree with a moisture-retentive mulch such as bark chips, old farmyard manure or well-rotted compost.

Halesia monticola

Amelanchier lamarckii
SNOWY MESPILUS

    Deciduous
    Height 10m [33ft]
    Spread 11m [36ft]
◆ Likes well-drained conditions
◆ Dislikes an alkaline soil
◆ In spring, pure white star-shaped flowers are followed by edible, purple-black fruit. Autumn leaf colour is excellent.

Camellia reticulata 'Captain Rawes'

    Evergreen
    Height 10m [33ft]
    Spread 5m [16ft]
◆ Grows well against a wall
◆ Dislikes an alkaline soil
◆ Large, semi-double, red-pink flowers appear in late spring

Halesia monticola
MOUNTAIN SNOWDROP TREE

    Deciduous
    Height 12m [40ft]
    Spread 8m [26ft]
◆ Prefers a neutral or acid soil
◆ Dislikes cold winds
◆ White, bell-shaped flowers are produced in spring, followed by green, winged fruit which persist throughout winter

one to impress the neighbours

Prunus 'Accolade'

Broussonetia papyrifera

Prunus 'Accolade'

ORNAMENTAL CHERRY

Deciduous

Height and spread 8m [26ft]

◆ Early flowering so needs a sheltered site
◆ Dislikes waterlogged soil
◆ Deep pink flower buds open as semi-double pink flowers with frilled petals

Rhododendron arboreum

TREE RHODODENDRON

Evergreen

Height 11m [36ft]

Spread 4m [13ft]

◆ Enjoys a site in shade
◆ Dislikes alkaline soil and waterlogging
◆ The large trusses of bell-shaped spring flowers may be pink or red. Each flower has black spots on the inside.

Broussonetia papyrifera

PAPER MULBERRY

Deciduous

Height and spread 8m [26ft]

◆ Prefers full sun
◆ Dislikes cold winds
◆ The male flowers appear as long yellow catkins, whereas the female flower is ball shaped with purple stigmas

Trees for summer time

On a hot day there is no shade to equal that provided by a large tree. The leaf canopy moves with the slightest breeze, cooling the air and lowering the temperature. This dappled shade, where light and shade mix, will help grass below the tree survive in summer.

In the glare of the sun, at the height of summer, foliage tends to lose its freshness and look dull. Trees that flower at this time provide colour and interest, while fragrance is a bonus hanging on the evening air.

Catalpa bignonioides 'Aurea'

Styrax japonicus

Catalpa bignonioides 'Aurea'
INDIAN BEAN TREE

  Deciduous
  Height and spread 10m [33ft]
- Enjoys a sheltered site in full sun
- Dislikes late spring frosts
- Large, golden, velvety leaves brighten the dullest garden. Pyramidal trusses of white flowers appear in summer.

Hoheria angustifolia

  Evergreen
  Height 7m [23ft]
  Spread 3m [10ft]
- Prefers an alkaline soil
- Dislikes a cold, biting wind
- The fragrant white flowers appear in profusion in late summer in time to tempt every butterfly for miles around.

Magnolia delavayi

  Evergreen
  Height 10m [33ft]
  Spread 9m [30ft]
- Grows well on a wall
- Tolerates an alkaline soil
- Parchment-like, creamy-white, fragrant flowers appear in late summer

one to impress the neighbours

Chionanthus virginicus

Styrax japonicus
JAPANESE SNOWBELL

Deciduous

Height 8m [26ft]

Spread 7m [23ft]

◆ Likes a sheltered spot

◆ Dislikes an alkaline soil

◆ This tree is good for autumn colour and, as a bonus, produces bell-shaped, creamy-white fragrant flowers in summer

Syringa pekinensis
LILAC

Deciduous

Height and spread 5m [16ft]

◆ Prefers an alkaline soil in full sun

◆ Dislikes hard pruning

◆ Large panicles of creamy-white flowers weigh down the branches in early summer

Chionanthus virginicus
AMERICAN FRINGE TREE

Deciduous

Height 4m [13ft]

Spread 3m [10ft]

◆ Likes a site in full sun

◆ Dislikes an alkaline soil

◆ The strange-looking fragrant white flowers look as if they have been shredded

Autumn trees

I love autumn. I love the brilliance of the leaf colours in every shade and hue. This is the time when green-leaved trees such as birch, hickory and poplar, which we take for granted all summer, suddenly turn to butter yellow. Autumn leaf colour may vary from tree to tree and be completely different in a range of soil types. Weather is also a major influence. Long, dry summers, and a lack of frost in autumn with no breeze to knock them off, will encourage the greenest of leaves to colour up, giving hues ranging from yellow through every shade of orange to brilliant reds and crimsons. The only sad thing about this season is that it has to end. Occasionally it seems to carry through into the early stages of winter, coming to an abrupt finish with a hard frost or torrential rain.

Late autumn is a good time to plant trees. The soil temperature hasn't dropped and there is the expectancy of plenty of rain over the winter: ideal conditions for planting evergreens. Bare-root deciduous trees may be planted and transplanted any time after they shed their foliage.

Malus 'John Downie'

Parrotia persica

Carya ovata
SHAGBARK HICKORY

Deciduous
Height 25m [80ft]
Spread 12m [40ft]
◆ Likes a rich soil with lots of humus
◆ Dislikes transplanting
◆ The brilliant golden autumn foliage follows interesting catkins in late spring

Cercidiphyllum japonicum
KATSURA TREE

Deciduous
Height 20m [66ft]
Spread 15m [50ft]
◆ Autumn leaf colour is better on an acid soil
◆ Dislikes cold, dry winds
◆ Fantastic leaf colouring in autumn, when the foliage smells of burnt sugar

Malus 'John Downie'
CRAB APPLE

Deciduous
Height 9m [30ft]
Spread 5m [16ft]
◆ Prefers a well-drained soil
◆ Dislikes late spring frost at flowering time
◆ Pink flower buds open to pure white apple blossom, followed by crab apples which change from yellow through red to scarlet

one to impress the neighbours

Sorbus sargentiana

Ostrya carpinifolia
HOP HORNBEAM

Deciduous
Height 20m [66ft]
Spread 15m [50ft]
◆ Tolerates sun or shade
◆ The foliage turns bright yellow in autumn at the same time as the pendulous, yellow male catkins appear

Parrotia persica
PERSIAN IRONWOOD

Deciduous
Height 8m [26ft]
Spread 10m [33ft]
◆ Prefers a well-drained soil in sun or light shade
◆ Autumn leaves progress through every shade of yellow, orange and red

Sorbus sargentiana
ROWAN TREE

Deciduous
Height and spread 10m [33ft]
◆ Prefers a neutral to acid soil rich in humus
◆ Dislikes deep shade
◆ The autumn leaves turn crimson, the clusters of berries are red and the large, sticky winter buds are red

Trees for winter display

Deciduous trees without their foliage look spectacular in winter, with the tracery of branches highlighted in frost or snow. Viewed against a watery winter sun they appear to be coated in gold. In contrast, evergreen trees add body to the winter landscape. Berries create interest when more showy summer flowering trees are exhausted. The bark of many acers, cherry and birch species is incredibly beautiful. But their full display isn't apparent as young trees and care must be taken not to plant shrubs around the trees that will later hide the effect.

Ilex aquifolium 'J. C. van Tol'

Acer davidii subsp. *grosseri*

Acer davidii subsp. grosseri
SNAKE-BARK MAPLE

Deciduous
Height and spread 14m [46ft]
◆ Dislikes wet soil
◆ The pale green bark is marked with lines of pure white. In autumn the foliage turns buttercup yellow.

Acer griseum
PAPER BARK MAPLE

Deciduous
Height and spread 9m [30ft]
◆ Tolerates most conditions
◆ The bark on older trees peels off to reveal the polished cinnamon young bark

Ilex aquifolium 'J. C. van Tol'
HOLLY

Evergreen
Height 7m [23ft]
Spread 4m [13ft]
◆ Needs full sun
◆ Dislikes dry soil
◆ Since – unusually for hollies – flowers of both sexes are on the same plant, this tree will carry a bumper crop of red berries

one to impress the neighbours

Acer griseum

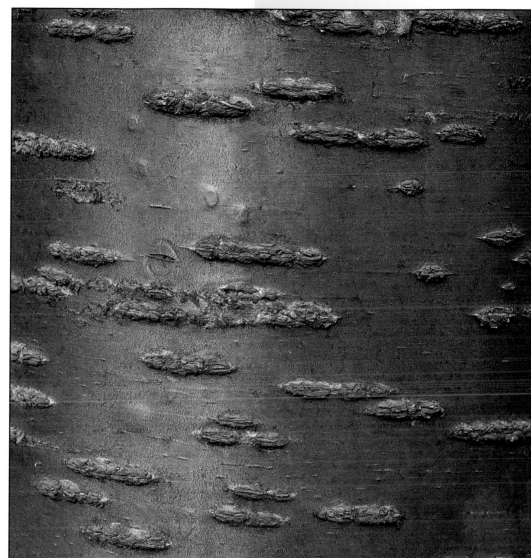

Prunus sargentii

Prunus x subhirtella 'Autumnalis'
WINTER-FLOWERING CHERRY

Deciduous
Height 8m [26ft]
Spread 7m [23ft]

◆ Prefers a well-drained soil in full sun
◆ Dislikes a cold, windy site
◆ The white semi-double flowers open from pink clusters of buds and will flower off and on from late autumn until late winter

Salix alba ssp. vitellina 'Britzensis'
WILLOW

Deciduous
Height 20m [66ft]
Spread 10m [33ft]

◆ Enjoys a hard pruning every second year
◆ Dislikes growing in shallow soil over chalk
◆ Grow this tree for its winter display when the younger branches are orange-red

Prunus sargentii

SARGENT'S CHERRY

Deciduous
Height and spread 15m [50ft]

◆ Likes a sunny site
◆ An all-year round favourite: good autumn leaf colour, icing-sugar pink flowers followed by deep crimson fruit, and bark to brighten the dullest winter day

Fruiting trees

There is something very satisfying about growing your own crops. Apples, pears, plums and peaches are worth growing to eat fresh from the tree.

Many fruit trees flower early in the spring, at a time when frost is common and a hard frost will damage or kill the blossom. If the weather is cold and wet there will be few insects to carry out pollination. Then there are hailstones and heavy rain that may damage the flowers or mark the young fruit. For these reasons, it is worthwhile giving fruiting trees the most favoured position in the garden, in a sheltered, sunny site. Avoid a spot that gets the morning sun, as a sudden thaw of frozen flowers will kill them before they set fruit.

Mespilus germanica

Castanea sativa

Castanea sativa
SPANISH CHESTNUT

Deciduous
Height 30m [100ft]
Spread 15m [50ft]
◆ Likes a long, hot summer
◆ Dislikes an infertile, sandy soil
◆ Trailing green catkins in spring give way to prickly shells containing the edible 'hot chestnuts'

Corylus avellana
HAZEL

Deciduous
Height and spread 5m [16ft]
◆ Prefers a well-drained alkaline soil in sun or light shade
◆ A cheerful winter display as well as a delicious fruit

Juglans regia
COMMON WALNUT

Deciduous
Height 30m [100ft]
Spread 20m [66ft]
◆ Likes a sheltered, sunny site
◆ Dislikes being transplanted
◆ The young foliage is orange, turning light brown before it becomes a deep glossy green for the summer

one to impress the neighbours

Cydonia oblonga

Mespilus germanica
MEDLAR

Deciduous
Height 5m [16ft]
Spread 8m [26ft]

◆ Succeeds in most soils
◆ Likes a sunny site
◆ Serving the fruit for dessert may not be the way to impress, since it is eaten after 'bletting', an Old English word for allowing it to rot. In spite of the smell it has a reasonable flavour, I'm told!

Morus nigra
BLACK MULBERRY

Deciduous
Height 12m [40ft]
Spread 13m [43ft]

◆ Likes a well drained soil in full sun
◆ Dislikes cold winds
◆ An attractive tree in fruit with green, red and purple berries all at the same time

Cydonia oblonga
QUINCE

Deciduous
Height and spread 5m [16ft]

◆ Fruits best in a site in full sun
◆ Dislikes hard pruning
◆ The pink or white spring flowers become large, fragrant, pear-shaped, golden yellow fruit

Berried treasures

Trees with berries and fruit are to be cherished. On the dullest day of winter, white, yellow, orange, pink, red or crimson berries will light up a tree. At the same time the food is welcomed by wildlife and, while it is frustrating to watch, you can not help but be amazed at the speed with which birds strip a tree of berries. The sight of a blackbird with its beak wedged impossibly wide trying to swallow a *Malus* 'Golden Hornet' crab apple is nature at its best.

The old saying that 'a large crop of berries means a hard winter ahead' is only a yarn. It is more likely to be the result of a good growing season the previous year.

Cotoneaster 'Cornubia'

Photinia davidiana

Cotoneaster 'Cornubia'

Semi-evergreen
Height and spread 6m [20ft]
- Prefers a sunny situation
- Dislikes cold winds
- This tree crops profusely every year with masses of bright red berries

Malus 'Red Sentinel'
CRAB APPLE

Deciduous
Height 7m [23ft]
Spread 6m [20ft]
- Dislikes late spring frosts
- The yellow-red apples quickly colour to a glossy deep red, lasting until well into the winter

Photinia davidiana

Evergreen
Height 8m [26ft]
Spread 5m [16ft]
- Prefers a well-drained site protected from drying winds
- The older leaves turn deep red in autumn, contrasting with the dark green of the young foliage. Bunches of crimson berries are produced all along the branches

one to impress the neighbours

Tetradium daniellii

Sorbus aucuparia 'Fructu Luteo'

MOUNTAIN ASH

Deciduous

Height 8m [26ft]

Spread 6m [20ft]

◆ Prefers a well-drained neutral or acid soil

◆ Masses of amber-yellow fruit are produced in clusters in early autumn

Sorbus vilmorinii

MOUNTAIN ASH

Deciduous

Height and spread 5m [16ft]

◆ Will tolerate shade

◆ Likes an acid soil

◆ Berries with a difference: they appear rose red, turn to clear pink and finally settle as white flushed with red

Tetradium daniellii

Deciduous

Height and spread 13m [42ft]

◆ Protect from cold winds

◆ Dislikes waterlogged soil

◆ Appearing in early autumn, the small, white flowers are followed by red berries that turn black

Variegation for variety

The foliage of many trees displays variegation. A variegated leaf surface has more than one colour – yellow and green being the most common combination. Cream-, pink- and white-leaved varieties occur with poplar and maple. Sometimes the margin of the leaf is edged in cream or white. In other species the green leaf may be marked on the surface with gold or cream.

Often variegated trees are the result of a 'sport' branch appearing on a normally green-leaved tree. The variegated stem is then rooted or grafted and a new variety is launched. Because of their origin, variegated trees tend to produce branches that revert to green leaves. Removing these all-green branches as they appear prevents the less vigorous, variegated part of the tree being swamped.

Ilex x altaclerensis 'Golden King'

Acer platanoides 'Drummondii'

Acer platanoides 'Drummondii'
VARIEGATED NORWAY MAPLE

Deciduous
Height and spread 11m [36ft]
◆ Cut out any green shoots immediately they appear
◆ Large, five-lobed 'maple' leaves are mid-green with a creamy-white margin.

Acer pseudoplatanus 'Leopoldii'
VARIEGATED SYCAMORE

Deciduous
Height and spread 10m [33ft]
◆ Tolerates most soil conditions
◆ Young foliage is pink, then a soft yellow, turning by midsummer to green splashed with pink and cream

Ilex x altaclerensis 'Golden King'
VARIEGATED HOLLY

Evergreen
Height 6m [20ft]
Spread 4m [13ft]
◆ Prefers a site in full sun
◆ Dislikes a dry soil
◆ The grey-green leaves have a broad gold margin, highlighting the bright red berries

one to impress the neighbours

Cornus controversa 'Variegata'

Liriodendron tulipifera 'Aureomarginatum'
VARIEGATED TULIP TREE

Deciduous

Height 18m [60ft]

Spread 10m [33ft]

◆ Prefers a neutral or acid soil

◆ Dislikes wet soil

◆ The early summer flowers are cup-shaped and pale green with an orange band around the base

Populus x candicans 'Aurora'
VARIEGATED BALM OF GILEAD

Deciduous

Height 13m [43ft]

Spread 6m [20ft]

◆ Dislikes waterlogged soil

◆ Needs to be pruned regularly

◆ The large, heart-shaped young leaves are splashed with white, cream and pink

Cornus controversa 'Variegata'
WEDDING CAKE TREE

Deciduous

Height and spread 7m [23ft]

◆ Dislikes waterlogged soil

◆ As well as good variegation there is the bonus of white summer flowers and blue-black berries in winter

Trees with ornamental bark

The full potential of tree bark is often ignored when deciding which trees to buy. At the time of selection, the bark of most young trees has nothing to show to suggest its future beauty. But there is a whole selection of trees with outstanding bark that warrant planting as specimens to show off their best asset.

Sometimes branches need to be removed to help the shape of the tree or lift the head. In trees grown for ornamental bark, they should be removed when small and as close to the trunk as possible to reduce scarring. It is normal for most gardeners to be able to identify mature, common trees from their bark. Ash, oak, beech, lime and birch are easily told apart.

Deciduous trees show their bark to best advantage after leaf fall. Evergreens such as eucalyptus shed their inner foliage, so displaying the patchwork bark on the branches as well as the main trunk.

Acer pensylvanicum 'Erythrocladum'

Arbutus menziesii

Acer pensylvanicum 'Erythrocladum'
STRIPPED MAPLE

Deciduous
Height and spread 10m [33ft]
◆ Dislikes deep shade
◆ Young shoots are pink, turning to red in winter. Older bark is orange-red with white striations

Acer tegmentosum

Deciduous
Height 8m [26ft]
Spread 9m [29ft]
◆ Dislikes cold winds
◆ Bright green and white striped bark is set off by the golden autumn leaf colour

Arbutus menziesii
MADRONA

Evergreen
Height and spread 13m [43ft]
◆ Prefers a sheltered site in full sun
◆ Dislikes alkaline soil
◆ Noted for its smooth, cinnamon-red bark, glossy dark green leaves and interesting flower and fruit

one to impress the neighbours

Stewartia pseudocamellia

Betula ermanii 'Greyswood Hill'
ERMAN'S BIRCH

Deciduous
Height 20m [66ft]
Spread 12m [40tt]

♦ Prefers a site in full sun
♦ Dislikes a waterlogged soil
♦ The young branches are orange-brown.
   Older bark is pink-white with brown
   lenticels

Eucalyptus pauciflora subsp. niphophila
SNOW GUM

Evergreen
Height and spread 6m [20ft]

♦ Prefers a neutral to acid soil
♦ Dislikes cold winds
♦ Mature bark is beautifully marked with
   blotches of green, grey and cream

Stewartia pseudocamellia

Deciduous
Height 18m [60ft]
Spread 7m [23 ft]

♦ Prefers an acid soil
♦ Dislikes cold winds
♦ The older bark flakes off, revealing a grey,
   brown and pale red patchwork effect

Trees for fragrance

Something that is enjoyable but not essential is described as a luxury. Perfume in the garden is one of those little luxuries that costs nothing extra. The scent may be subtle or overpowering but there is always the urge to find the source. Fragrant flowers and aromatic foliage may both be employed to provide the pleasure. Evergreen trees with aromatic foliage are especially welcome in winter, when a crushed handful of foliage can bring back memories.

Magnolia kobus

Luma apiculata

Eucryphia x intermedia 'Rostrevor'

Evergreen
Height 10m [33ft]
Spread 6m [20ft]

◆ Prefers a moist acid soil
◆ Dislikes cold winds
◆ In mid to late summer the fragrant, single, pure white flowers bend the branches

Hamamelis mollis
CHINESE WITCH HAZEL

Deciduous
Height and spread 4m [13ft]

◆ Prefers a moist, well-drained, acid soil in full sun
◆ One of the best for winter fragrance

Luma apiculata
MYRTLE

Evergreen
Height 6m [20ft]
Spread 4m [13ft]

◆ Needs a well-drained soil in full sun
◆ Dislikes cold winds
◆ The dull dark leaves contrast with the cinnamon-coloured bark and are highly aromatic

one to impress the neighbours

Cladrastis lutea

Magnolia kobus

Deciduous
Height 12m [40ft]
Spread 9m [30ft]
◆ Will grow on alkaline soil
◆ Dislikes a dry soil
◆ The foliage is aromatic and, as a bonus, the large, pure white, spring flowers are fragrant

Malus 'Profusion'
CRAB APPLE

Deciduous
Height and spread 9m [30ft]
◆ Grows best in full sun
◆ Dislikes waterlogged soil
◆ In late spring the deep purple-pink blossom exudes a light fragrance

Cladrastis lutea

Deciduous
Height 12m [40ft]
Spread 9m [30ft]
◆ Needs full sun
◆ Dislikes strong wind as the branches are brittle
◆ Panicles of fragrant white flowers trail down in early summer, resembling wisteria. Autumn colour is good, too.

Weeping trees

Of all the tree shapes available, I think I prefer those of a pendulous habit. Small weeping trees are compact and manageable. Large specimens, including ash and beech, have a flowing outline and appear graceful compared to bolder, upright and spreading trees.

Many varieties are budded or grafted on to upright growing species and are prone to grow shoots below the joint. These stronger growing shoots must be removed to prevent the grafted variety being overpowered. Occasionally plants will be available which have been grafted higher up the stem of the rootstock than the normal 2m [6ft 6in]. This allows the pendulous or weeping branches to trail fauther before reaching the ground. It is particularly effective with weeping ash.

Fagus sylvatica 'Purpurea Pendula'

Betula pendula 'Youngii'

Betula pendula 'Youngii'
YOUNG'S WEEPING BIRCH

> Deciduous
> Height 8m [26ft]
> Spread 4m [13ft]

- Will grow in full sun or partial shade
- Dislikes a dry soil
- In time this tree forms a domed head. With the leaves turning yellow in autumn it resembles a yellow mushroom

Fagus sylvatica 'Purpurea Pendula'
WEEPING PURPLE BEECH

> Deciduous
> Height and spread 3m [10ft]

- Needs full sun
- Tolerates most soils except waterlogged conditions
- The glossy deep purple foliage trails down to ground level on thin stems

Fraxinus excelsior 'Pendula'
WEEPING ASH

> Deciduous
> Height 15m [50ft]
> Spread 8m [26ft]

- Prefers an alkaline soil
- Dislikes wet soil
- The trailing branches of this ash are stiff and quickly reach the ground. The bare stems in winter look combed

one to impress the neighbours

Tilia petiolaris

Prunus 'Cheal's Weeping'

Deciduous
Height and spread 3m[10ft]
◆ Needs full sun
◆ Dislikes waterlogged soil
◆ The branches arch gently, forming a broad
  umbrella shape laden, in early spring, with
  double, bright pink flowers

Pyrus salicifolia 'Pendula'
WEEPING SILVER PEAR

Deciduous
Height 5m [16ft]
Spread 4m [13ft]
◆ Tolerates most soils
◆ Dislikes a shady site
◆ The young leaves are silvery grey, turning
  to a grey-green as they age

Tilia petiolaris
WEEPING SILVER LIME

Deciduous
Height 30m [100ft]
Spread 18m [60ft]
◆ Prefers an alkaline soil
◆ Dislikes cold winds
◆ The dark green leaves are white on the
  underside, reflecting the sun as they
  move. Fragrant yellow flowers appear in
  late summer

CONIFERS IN THE GARDEN

Conifers add colour, shape, texture and, frequently, aromatic foliage to any garden. It is to their credit that most of them are evergreen, making a display for all 12 months. Those that are not, such as the Japanese and European larches, try very hard to make up for their shortcomings. Before leaf fall they turn soft, honey yellow and in early spring, before most deciduous trees are awake, their bright, fresh green foliage coats the branches.

Some detractors point to the insignificant flowers of conifers, but there are few seed pods to equal the magic of a pine cone or the blue, upright, candle-like cones decorating *Abies koreana*. The word conifer is derived from the Latin *conus*, a cone, and *ferre*, to carry or bear, and in many such trees the cones are their most attractive feature.

Conifer bark is as diverse as the plants themselves and as attractive and interesting as any displayed by deciduous trees.

An excellent example of the year-round value of conifers. This swamp cypress (*Taxodium distichum*) is classic green in spring and summer (left), burnt gold in autumn (right) and, with a little help from the weather, brown with a touch of white frosting in winter (opposite).

SIZE MATTERS

In the past, conifers got a bad press and many gardeners were disappointed with them. The root cause was poor or bad labelling, with slow-growing species and varieties being sold as dwarf plants. A true dwarf species, such as *Juniperus communis* 'Compressa', whose maximum height is about 80cm (32in), will, in a short time, be swamped by *Chamaecyparis lawsoniana* 'Ellwoodii', for example, which was often sold as a dwarf variety when its actual habit is slow-growing and its full height as much as 8m (26ft).

Ground-covering conifers will travel for metres, rooting as they go. In the right site with lots of room to ramble, they are excellent. Wrongly planted, in an inadequate space, they are nothing but trouble, smothering all that stands in their way.

Large conifers need thinking about and it is not a good idea to plant a potential monster just because you like it. By all means plant a specimen, but make sure space allows it to grow to its heart's content. Then it will give you decades of pleasure and you'll be secure in the knowledge that it will still be flourishing in a few hundred years. The secret of success lies in leaving the allocated space unplanted, with nothing to crowd and squeeze the tree.

FINDING THE SPACE

There is no garden too small for conifers. Many will grow for years in the confines of a stone trough. True dwarf varieties are happy in containers. Slow-growing conifers will add shape and texture to mixed shrub beds.

Underplanting conifers with suitably sized plants can provide carpets of colour. One of the traditional and most successful combinations is a mixed conifer and heather planting, using autumn-, winter- and spring-flowering heather species.

Thuja orientalis 'Aurea Nana' is a well-behaved little tree that will grace any sunny or lightly shaded site – and you won't have to worry about it outgrowing its welcome.

Specimen weeping plants are spectacular planted in grass. For winter colour on a grand scale, you can't improve on the display of blue and gold foliage from a mixed planting of towering conifers.

PLANTING

Unlike deciduous trees, evergreens are active and growing all year. They slow down in winter but still draw in water and transpire through the foliage. This is worth remembering when planting and transplanting.

Small container-grown conifers may be planted at any time of year, providing the root ball is moist and the planting hole is wet. A square planting hole slightly deeper than the root ball will encourage the plant's roots to spread out instead of continuing to curl round in the shape of the ball. Tease out the roots prior to planting so that they will grow into the surrounding soil.

Larger plants and those to be transplanted should be moved in spring or autumn when the soil is warm. This aids rooting and there is also a good chance of rain to reduce excess transpiration. Keep the root area well watered for the first season but avoid waterlogging the soil.

When a stake is needed to prevent the tree leaning, use a short one. Position the tree tie close to the ground to hold the stem: this allows the head of the conifer to move with the wind and strengthen the roots and trunk.

PRUNING

Many conifers benefit from pruning. Those plants grown for their juvenile foliage sometimes produce branches which have reverted to the original adult foliage of the parent plant. If these are not cut out as soon as you spot them, they will eventually weaken the tree and the whole plant will revert.

Some young trees are prone to producing double leaders. Removing the weaker shoot is necessary to keep the shape of the plant.

Most conifers will not produce new growth if pruned hard, as they usually have only an outer shell of evergreen foliage. The centre is brown and dead, so where green foliage has died, it won't regrow. The exceptions to this rule are yew, a few junipers and the fast-growing leyland cypress. Even when cut to the stump yew will survive and regrow as good as ever. Cypresses will withstand being severely reduced in height, growing away again to become an equally tall problem.

Conifer hedges and topiary shapes will only be maintained if they are regularly clipped to build up a dense, tight mass of leafy twigs.

For more information on pruning and training, see pages 80–83, and for topiary, see pages 106–107.

FLOWERS AND CONES

The male flowers of a conifer are usually shaped like either a catkin or a cone. They are often referred to as male cones but are, in fact, clusters of flowers. Female cones start out as clusters of flowers, hardening up into cones to hold the young seed. A cone may be thought of as the fruit or berry of the conifer. Yew and juniper do actually produce single-seed berries rather than cones.

In some conifers the seed takes a year to mature. Others may take up to two years before the cone opens to release the seed.

All too often the flowers of the conifer are taken for granted. Sometimes they are small and not conspicuous or they are high up on the tree and out of sight. Usually they are beautiful in shape and colour. Many of the flowers are bright red or yellow and they may take the form of pendulous catkins or cones. Most conifers produce their flowers, both male and female, in spring, but cedars flower in early autumn, when the male flowers release clouds of yellow pollen.

The fruits – or cones – of conifers can be just as eye-catching as the berries of other trees. This variety of the Korean fir (*Abies koreana flava*) produces handsome candle-like cones very early on in its life.

Conifers for clay soil

Sequoia sempervirens 'Prostrata'

Cryptomeria japonica 'Elegans'
JAPANESE CEDAR

Height 8m [26ft]

Spread 5m [16ft]

◆ Prefers a sheltered site

◆ Dislikes waterlogged soil

◆ Pale green foliage is soft to the touch, contrasting with the orange-cinnamon peeling bark. Foliage turns purple in winter

Larix kaempferi
JAPANESE LARCH

Deciduous

Height 30m [100ft]

Spread 6m [20ft]

◆ Dislikes a dry, chalky soil

◆ Spring foliage is blue-green, turning to orange-yellow in autumn with red-purple winter shoots

Metasequoia glyptostroboides
DAWN REDWOOD

Deciduous

Height 30m [100ft]

Spread 7m [23ft]

◆ Dislikes a dry soil

◆ New bright green leaves turn to deep pink and finally a golden-brown before falling

Chamaecyparis thyoides 'Ericoides'
WHITE FALSE CYPRESS

Height 2m [6ft 6in]

Spread 1m [3ft]

◆ Dislikes alkaline soil

◆ Foliage turns a deep plum-purple in winter

Sequoia sempervirens 'Prostrata'

Height 2m [6ft 6in]

Spread 3m [10ft]

◆ Likes a position in full sun

◆ Red-brown horizontal shoots carry double rows of bright, glaucous green leaves

Conifers for dry sandy soil

Cedrus deodara 'Golden Horizon'
GOLDEN DEODAR CEDAR

Height 2m [6ft 6in]

Spread 7m [23ft]

◆ Dislikes heavy, wet ground

◆ Sulphur-yellow leaves become yellowish-green in winter or if grown in shade

Ginkgo biloba

Height 20m [66ft]

Spread 5m [16ft]

Deciduous

◆ Prefers a site in full sun

◆ This tree was growing more than 160 million years ago and its notched leaves with fan-shaped veins haven't changed since then

Juniperus scopulorum 'Skyrocket'

Height 6m [20ft]

Spread 1m [3ft]

◆ Grows best in a dry atmosphere in a well-drained soil

◆ Small, pointed grey-green leaves give this narrow, upright tree an austere look

Pinus strobus
WEYMOUTH PINE

Height 30m [100ft]

Spread 8m [26ft]

◆ Dislikes waterlogged, alkaline soil

◆ Female cones change from green to dark brown and become curved

Thuja occidentalis 'Rheingold'

Height 4m [13ft]

Spread 3m [10ft]

◆ Plant in an open site for the best winter colour

◆ This conifer produces juvenile and adult foliage, and both root easily to form different-shaped plants with golden-yellow foliage

The butter-yellow autumn colour of *Ginkgo biloba*

Conifers for acid soil

Chamaecyparis lawsoniana 'Minima Aurea'

Chamaecyparis lawsoniana 'Minima Aurea'

Height 2m [6ft 6in]

Spread 1m [3ft]

◆ Prefers a sunny site

◆ Eventually forms a rounded dome of firm golden-yellow foliage ideal for a fairy to sit on

Chamaecyparis pisifera 'Boulevard'

Height 8m [26ft]

Spread 3m [10ft]

◆ Grows best in moist soil in full sun

◆ In summer the silver-blue foliage is wonderfully soft, becoming grey-green with a purple tinge in winter

Chamaecyparis pisifera 'Filifera Aurea'

Height 8m [26ft]

Spread 6m [20ft]

◆ Dislikes a dry soil and full sun

◆ Thin, thread-like, bright yellow foliage deepens to golden-yellow in winter

Picea breweriana

BREWER SPRUCE

Height 15m [50ft]

Spread 4m [13ft]

◆ Prefers a well-drained soil in full sun

◆ Long, curved, trailing branches carry large green cones in pairs, which turn purple and then red-brown

Tsuga canadensis 'Pendula'

EASTERN HEMLOCK

Height 2m [6ft 6in]

Spread 8m [26ft]

◆ Prefers a well-drained, humus-rich soil

◆ Dislikes cold, drying winds

◆ Soft mid-green foliage carpets the ground, hugging any obstacle in its way

Conifers for alkaline soil

Juniperus communis 'Hibernica'
IRISH JUNIPER

    Height 5m [16ft]

    Spread 60cm [2ft]

◆ Succeeds in most soil types

◆ Makes a great columnar shape in the
garden

◆ Small light green foliage becomes
darker in winter

Juniperus horizontalis
CREEPING JUNIPER

    Height 30cm [1ft]

    Spread indefinite

◆ Enjoys a well-drained, sunny site

◆ Leaf colour may vary from light green
through grey-green to a bluish green

Picea omorika
SERBIAN SPRUCE

    Height 25m [80ft]

    Spread 3m [10ft]

◆ Tolerates dry, impoverished soil

◆ Blue-black cones turn a beautiful
cinnamon-red when mature

Taxus baccata 'Fastigiata'
IRISH YEW

Height 13m [43ft]

Spread 7m [23ft]

◆ Loves a damp climate

◆ Produces bright red berries that stand
out against black-green foliage

Taxus baccata 'Summergold'

    Height 75cm [30in]

    Spread 8m [26ft]

◆ Tolerates an impoverished soil

◆ Bright, golden summer foliage turns to
dark green with a yellow margin in winter

Juniperus horizontalis

Windbreak conifers

A mixed evergreen planting of conifers including *Pinus sylvestris* grown as a shelter belt

Chamaecyparis lawsoniana 'Kilmacurragh'

Height 12m [40ft]

Spread 5m [16ft]

◆ Prefers a well-drained, acid soil

◆ The Irish answer to the Italian cypress with foliage that changes from bright green to dark green as it ages.

x Cuprocyparis leylandii 'Robinson's Gold'

GOLDEN LEYLAND CYPRESS

Height 25m [80ft]

Spread 6m [20ft]

◆ Grows best in a deep, well-drained soil.

◆ A great tree in the right setting with bright, golden foliage, turning deep gold in winter.

Larix decidua

EUROPEAN LARCH, COMMON LARCH

Deciduous

Height 30m [100ft]

Spread 20m [66ft]

◆ Prefers a well-drained soil

◆ Dislikes alkaline soil

◆ Soft, pale green foliage in spring, becoming bright green and turning a soft yellow-brown in autumn

Picea sitchensis

SITKA SPRUCE

Height 50m [166ft]

Spread 12m [40ft]

◆ Prefers an acid soil in full sun

◆ Female cones are green turning to a soft yellow-brown as they mature

Pinus sylvestris

SCOTS PINE

Height 30m [100ft]

Spread 9m [30ft]

◆ Prefers a well-drained soil in full sun

◆ Male flowers are a bright orange-red, contrasting with the blue-green needles

Hedging conifers

Chamaecyparis lawsoniana 'Lutea'

Height 15m [50ft]

Spread 4m [13ft]

◆ Prefers a sunny site.

◆ Slow growing with flattened sprays of bright, golden-yellow foliage

Taxus baccata
ENGLISH YEW

Height 15m [50ft]

Spread 10m [33ft]

◆ Grows well in a sunny or shaded site

◆ Leaves are dark green, paler green on the underside and female plants produce bright red berries

Thuja orientalis 'Aurea Nana'

Height 1.6m [5ft]

Spread 1m [3ft]

◆ Grows well on acid or alkaline soil providing it isn't waterlogged

◆ Ferny foliage is butter-yellow in summer, becoming a bronze-yellow in cold areas in winter

Thuja plicata 'Atrovirens'
WESTERN RED CEDAR

Height 15m [50ft]

Spread 5m [16ft]

◆ Tolerates heavy, wet soil

◆ When crushed, the glossy, dark green leaves are wonderfully fragrant

Tsuga heterophylla
WESTERN HEMLOCK

Height 30m [100 ft]

Spread 10m [33ft]

◆ Tolerates shade but dislikes cold winds

◆ Glossy, dark green leaves have white bands on the underside

Classic elegance is the keynote of this traditional yew hedge

Conifers for small gardens

Picea abies 'Clanbrassiliana'

Height 2m [6ft 6in]
Spread 3m [10ft]

◆ Prefers a moist soil
◆ Dislikes an alkaline soil
◆ Beautiful red-brown winter buds stand out against the mid-green foliage

Pinus mugo 'Pumilio'
DWARF MOUNTAIN PINE

Height 2m [6ft 6in]
Spread 3m [10ft]

◆ Prefers a dry soil.
◆ Tolerates an alkaline soil
◆ If grown from seed there is a great variation in this plant but all forms have long conspicuous winter buds

Taxus baccata 'Fastigiata Aureomarginata'
GOLDEN IRISH YEW

Height 6m [20ft]
Spread 3m [10ft]

◆ Prefers a well-drained soil in full sun
◆ A superb upright yew with leaves edged in bright golden-yellow

Pinus mugo 'Pumilio'

Chamaecyparis obtusa 'Nana'
HINOKI CYPRESS

Height 60cm [2ft]
Spread 90cm [3ft]

◆ Prefers a moist soil
◆ Dislikes cold winds
◆ A great wee dwarf conifer for planting in a rockery or a container

Juniperus communis 'Compressa'
NOAH'S ARK JUNIPER

Height 80cm [32in]
Spread 45cm [18in]

◆ Dislikes cold, frosty weather
◆ Forms an amazingly dense, compact plant with mid-green leaves. A true dwarf variety.

Conifers for medium gardens

Abies koreana
KOREAN FIR

> Height 10m [33ft]
>
> Spread 6m [20ft]

- Enjoys cold weather
- Prefers an alkaline soil
- Produces masses of deep blue or purple, upright, candle-like cones from an early age

Chamaecyparis lawsoniana 'Columnaris'

> Height 10m [33ft]
>
> Spread 1m [3ft]

- Dislikes cold winds
- Forms an upright column of blue-green, turning a duller green in winter

Chamaecyparis lawsoniana 'Ellwoodii'

> Height 8m [26ft]
>
> Spread 2m [6ft 6in]

- Dislikes waterlogged soil
- Grey-green leaves turn to blue-green in winter

Chamaecyparis lawsoniana 'Pembury Blue'

> Height 15m [50ft]
>
> Spread 3m [10ft]

- Tolerates light shade
- New growths are bright blue, fading to a silver-blue as the leaves age

Picea pungens 'Koster'
KOSTER'S BLUE SPRUCE

> Height 10m [33ft]
>
> Spread 5m [16ft]

- Prefers a deep, well-drained soil in full sun
- New leaves are bright blue, the older leaves become green-blue

Chamaecyparis lawsoniana 'Ellwoodii'

Conifers for large gardens

Cunninghamia lanceolata
CHINA FIR

> Height 20m [66ft]
>
> Spread 6m [20ft]

◆ Prefers a well-drained soil

◆ Dislikes shallow ground

◆ The long, bright green, pointed leaves have two white lines on the underside

Juniperus squamata 'Meyeri'

> Height 8m [26ft]
>
> Spread 3m [10ft]

◆ Tolerates drought conditions

◆ In China it is locally known as the 'fish tail juniper'. I have no idea why.

Pinus ponderosa
WESTERN YELLOW PINE

> Height 35m [116ft]
>
> Spread 8m [26ft]

◆ Tolerates cold winds

◆ Prefers an open, sunny site

Podocarpus salignus
WILLOW LEAF PODOCARP

> Height 20m [66ft]
>
> Spread 8m [26ft]

◆ Prefers a site in full sun with shelter from cold winds

◆ This conifer looks more like an evergreen willow. The cone is really a purple-red fruit with a nut inside.

Thuja occidentalis
WHITE CEDAR

> Height 20m [66ft]
>
> Spread 4m [13ft]

◆ Prefers a moist, well-drained soil in full sun

◆ When crushed the pale green leaves smell of apples

Cunninghamia lanceolata

Specimen conifers

Cedrus atlantica 'Glauca Pendula'
WEEPING BLUE ATLAS CEDAR

Height up to 3m [10ft]

Spread 4m [13ft]

◆ Tolerates a dry soil

◆ Trained with an upright central leader before it is allowed to weep, it makes a magnificent specimen tree

Cedrus libani 'Sargentii'

Height 80cm [32in]

Spread 4m [13ft]

◆ Prefers a well-drained soil

◆ Ideal for planting in a rockery with its blue-green leaves

Cupressus macrocarpa 'Goldcrest'
GOLDEN MONTEREY CYPRESS

Height 5m [16ft]

Spread 2.5m [8ft]

◆ Prefers a well-drained soil

◆ Dislikes cold winds

◆ Feathery foliage turns to a buttery-yellow in winter

Juniperus chinensis 'Spartan'
CHINESE JUNIPER

Height 10m [33ft]

Spread 1.2m [4ft]

◆ Succeeds in a poor, dry soil

◆ Peculiar in having both juvenile and adult dark green foliage

Taxodium distichum
SWAMP CYPRESS

Deciduous

Height 30m [100ft]

Spread 8m [26ft]

◆ Prefers a wet soil in sun or partial shade

◆ Female cones are green turning to black; pendant male cones are red

Cedrus atlantica 'Glauca Pendula'

TREES
GROW ON YOU

A tree isn't just for a season: it's for life. With care and attention, most trees should have a long life – some of them will outlive not only you but your grandchildren as well. They are always growing, even though in later years this is less noticeable. Before buying, take the trouble to check out a mature version of the tree you plan to buy – at a park or public garden. Then you will know what yours is going to look like in the fullness of time. The planting site must be selected with thought to the future and the ultimate size of the tree. Will it become too large for the space, cast shade, block a view, annoy neighbours or be a danger to property?

The ultimate spread of branches and roots will have a bearing on your choice of position. The spread on either side of the trunk of a mature chestnut may be as much as 20m (66ft). On a lesser scale, cherry tree roots will work their way to the surface, damaging lawns and making mowing difficult. Where the landscape design calls for more than one tree, plant them sufficiently far apart to prevent them growing into one another, which would spoil their shape. The exception to this rule is when the end result is to be a shelter belt or windbreak, in which case close spacing is to be encouraged, allowing the branches of individual trees to intertwine and filter out the wind.

The tree's site will affect the level of maintenance. If planting in grass, keep a 60–100cm (2–3ft) circle around the base of the tree free from weeds and grass to prevent competition for water and nutrients. This will also reduce the risk of the base of the trunk being damaged by the lawnmower or strimmer. In any case, in later years the head of the tree will cast shade and the soil underneath will be dry, making it difficult to grow anything below it (for exceptions to this rule, see page 112–13).

The juxtaposition of trees and dwelling is often over-emphasised. Most of the smaller garden trees may be planted beside modern properties with no risk from roots or branches, though poplar and willow do have roots that travel far and wide, damaging pipework and old, weak foundations. More

serious causes for concern are the problems of shrinkage and heave, which are particularly prevalent on clay soil. If roots absorb too much of the available moisture, the underlying clay shrinks, causing foundations to settle. If the trees are then felled, more moisture is left in the ground, allowing the clay to expand and lift the foundations. I would recommend that, on a heavy, plastic clay soil, you avoid planting trees such as poplars which will eventually have a large, aggressive root system. Where such mature trees exist, they should – given the choice – be removed before construction, rather than after the house has been built.

When looking at a majestic specimen tree it is worth remembering that it started life in a small way and was, for many years, vulnerable to the ravages of pests, diseases, larger animals and even man. As the years progressed and the tree grew sufficiently large to withstand most pests it became more dependent on soil type, nutrients and water, all of which were sourced by its roots. These had to travel deep and wide through soil undisturbed since the Ice Age. Yes, it's true that large oaks from small acorns grow – but many don't make it.

Soil

Some species of trees are fussy regarding soil type, preferring acid, alkaline, wet, dry or whatever (see Six of the Best, page 18, and the Directory, page 114, for specific guidance). Others are more obliging and thrive in a range of conditions. Birch, for instance, will succeed in acid or alkaline soil, clay or peat.

Some species will do well no matter how inhospitable the soil and climatic conditions. That is not to say that conditions shouldn't be improved. I recommend adding humus to soil in the form of rotted farmyard manure, compost, leaf mould or composted bark mulch. This will open up the worst clay or help to retain moisture in a free-draining soil. Bonemeal may be added along with the manure or compost. This is a slow-release fertiliser that becomes available to the tree through the roots over a period of months.

Trees don't have 'off days' – this horse chestnut (*Aesculus hippocastanum* 'Baumannii') is magnificent even in the depths of winter.

Planting a tree

Unlike herbaceous plants and some shrubs, a tree is a long-term plant. With luck it won't ever need to be moved, which means that planting time is your best opportunity to give the plant roots what they want, and you should make the most of it.

1 Make the planting hole larger than the root area of the tree. Keep the top-soil in a separate pile to the subsoil – you will know when you hit subsoil as it is harder and poorer. Fork up the base of the hole, allowing water to drain and the roots to penetrate the subsoil. Don't unwrap the roots until you are ready to plant or they will dry out.

2 Place the tree in the hole, making sure that there is enough room to spread out the roots. Where a stake is needed (see 7, below), work out the best position so that it won't interfere with the roots. Remove the tree before you drive in the stake to avoid damaging the roots.

5 Mix a couple of handfuls (90-180g/3-6oz) of bonemeal and some old farmyard manure into the topsoil. Backfill around the roots, shaking the tree to settle the soil. Firm the soil with your foot to exclude air pockets, and tread the surface around the tree down into a dish shape so that water does not run off before it has time to penetrate the soil.

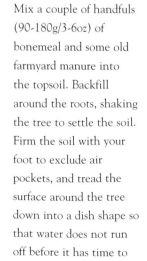

6 Water well after planting to settle the soil around the roots. For the first season keep the soil in the vicinity of the roots well watered and spray the foliage to prevent the tree from drying out and wilting.

3 Spread a layer of rotted farmyard manure in the base of the hole – it gets the trees off to a good start and retains moisture when they need it. Cover with 15cm (6in) of topsoil.

4 Put the tree back in the hole and spread out the roots. Prune any broken roots back to healthy tissue, taking care not to damage the small fibrous roots. Plant the tree at the same depth as before – there will be an obvious soil mark on the bark to guide you.

7 Use a strap and pad to hold the tree firmly to a timber stake. A short stake tied at a height of 60cm (24in) will allow the tree to move in the wind while the root is held steady. The movement will thicken the tree trunk so that after a short time it will be able to stand without support.

RIGHT Small trees may not need to be staked but those with a large head of branches or large specimen trees are likely to blow out of the ground if they are not supported with a stake and tie.

Planting a whip

Small whips – young trees usually available from nurseries as bare-root plants – are easier to plant than standards, but it still makes sense to do the job properly. They may be planted without digging a proper hole.

1 Instead use a spade: push it into the soil, lever it backwards and then lift it out, leaving a slit to hold the roots.

2 Slip the roots of the whip in and firm with your foot to seal the hole.

Transplanting

There are occasions when it is necessary to transplant trees. You may be moving house and want to bring a tree of sentimental value with you. Before the sale is agreed it is essential that you provide your estate agent or solicitor with a list of plants you intend to remove. If a favourite tree can't be moved until later in the season, an understanding buyer may allow you to return at the proper time to dig it up.

Trees may also have to be moved to allow an extension to be built. If they have been spaced incorrectly and are in competition, one will have to be moved before both trees are damaged.

Deciduous trees may be lifted and replanted from late autumn to early spring, depending on the soil conditions. Evergreens are best moved in mid-autumn when the soil is still warm, or alternatively in mid-spring when the ground is warming up. The larger the tree, the more difficult it is to lift it with its roots intact. There comes a point where the amount of work needed to prepare the tree for transplanting does not justify the effort or expense.

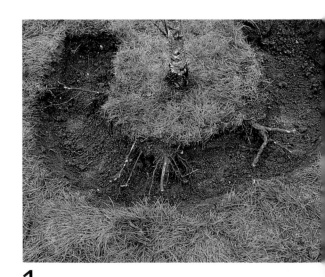

1 Even large trees may be lifted successfully but, where time allows, it is best to prepare them the year before. Excavate a 30cm (12in) trench around the tree 60-100cm (24-40in) away from the trunk and cut through any roots.

3 Mulch around the collar
of the tree to retain the
moisture in the soil and
help prevent weeds
growing in competition.

2 Fill the trench with a mixture of soil and
compost to encourage new fibrous roots to
grow into the area. The tree may be lifted
the next year after the root area has been
well watered. Prepare the new planting
hole before lifting the tree.

Watering

Watering should be done properly. That means applying
enough water to soak the soil thoroughly. Use a spade
to check that the soil is wet to a considerable depth and
not just the top 5cm (2in). Shallow watering encourages the roots to stay near the surface instead of going
deep in search of water. Deep roots are desirable as they
seek out nutrients and trace elements, as well as
anchoring the tree upright in a storm.

Feeding

I am a great believer in feeding young trees and leaving
the older trees to their own devices. Young trees will
benefit from an annual feed using a slow-release
fertiliser. Apply it in spring, washing it into the surface
of the soil in a circle at least as large as the spread of
the branches. When applied at the recommended
dosage (read the instructions on the package), the
fertiliser will be released into the soil over a period of
up to nine months. This type of fertiliser works on the
principle of osmatic pressure. Moisture enters through
the outer shell of the fertiliser granule, dissolving the
nutrients and releasing them into the soil. During
periods of dry weather the action stops through a lack
of moisture.

Nitrogen fertilisers encourage fast, soft growth that
will be liable to frost damage later in the year. By
contrast, high levels of potash in a fertiliser will harden
growths and encourage flowers, berries and fruit.
Phosphate encourages a good root system. Applying a
balanced fertiliser that incorporates these three main
nutrients will ensure sturdy growth.

Training and pruning

A well-behaved tree may make good growth each year, but it still needs a helping hand to produce a balanced shape that is pleasing to the eye, with no crossing branches or congestion. This is where training and pruning come in.

The most important pruning is that undertaken when the tree is young. The ultimate shape of a mature tree is often decided by the framework of branches formed at this time. A satisfactory shape may be achieved quite quickly, but pruning may be necessary to encourage the new shoots to head in the right direction. For extra information on pruning conifers, see page 63.

Many of our better-known garden trees have been trained by pruning into an artificial habit and require maintenance to retain their shape. Standard and half-standard trees (see page 16), such as cherry, rowan, crab apple and laburnum, have had the side shoots removed from the main stem so that the tree forms a 'head' at the required height. Some trees may have been grafted on to a different rootstock at the desired height and allowed to grow on from that point. Birch and alder will usually form feathered trees, with branches up the stem from ground level, although as the tree ages these may be shed. Conifers and hollies form a similar shape but always retain their side branches.

Multi-stemmed trees such as magnolias behave in the same way as large shrubs, producing lots of branches at, or close to, the base. However, some multi-stemmed species, such as *Cotoneaster* 'Cornubia', may be trained as a standard instead. To do this, remove all but one of the branches and train the single stem up a stake. Allow a branched head to form when the stem reaches 2m (6ft 6in). The end result is an impressive well-shaped tree that shows off its display of red berries.

When to prune

Mature deciduous trees are easier to prune in winter when the leaves have fallen. The exceptions are cherry and plum trees, which should be pruned in summer. Both are prone to silver leaf disease, which can kill a tree. The spores of this disease are dormant in summer, so there is less risk of infection through the fresh wounds if the trees are in leaf.

All trees are prone to 'bleed' if pruned in the spring when the sap is rising. Some species, notably birch, have a powerful capillary action, causing them to drip badly when cut. The cut branch may drip for weeks, weakening the tree and increasing the risk of disease.

General guidelines

When pruning, always use sharp tools. Small branches can be cut with a knife or secateurs. Larger branches up to 5cm (2in) in diameter can be removed or shortened using a pair of long-armed pruners.

Use a chain saw or hand saw to remove large main limbs. Cut partway through on the underside of the branch first. The weight of the limb will pull the branch down and, without the preliminary undercut, it would rip the bark right down the trunk. Then make the main cut in line with the branch collar where the limb joins the main trunk. Finally use a sharp knife to trim any ragged edges of bark, leaving a smooth wound that will soon callus over with new bark.

Where a tree is planted in grass, remove any very low branches for ease of mowing. Remember, pruning promotes growth. The amount you prune off will regrow elsewhere on the tree.

Shaping the framework

The results of spending a few minutes shaping the framework of a young tree will still be evident years later. There are three golden rules for success:

1 Prune out weak or diseased branches first.

2 If two branches are rubbing, cut off the weaker, diseased or most misshapen branch.

3 Where two main stems meet, avoid a narrow angle that will be a weak point vulnerable to splitting when the tree is older. Cut off the branch that is most angled.

Directing a shoot

There is a simple principle for getting a shoot to grow where you would like it to. Choose a growth bud that is pointing in the direction you want the stem to grow. Growth buds are usually thin and pointed – flower buds on the same tree will be fatter. Cut the shoot back to just above the chosen bud. A bud on the upper side of the shoot will

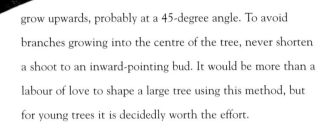

grow upwards, probably at a 45-degree angle. To avoid branches growing into the centre of the tree, never shorten a shoot to an inward-pointing bud. It would be more than a labour of love to shape a large tree using this method, but for young trees it is decidedly worth the effort.

Rejuvenating an old tree

The effect of pruning in stimulating a tree into growth can be used to bring a new lease of life to a neglected tree. Some trees are more tolerant of severe pruning than others, and these include elm, horse chestnut, lime, mulberry, oak, poplar and yew. Even cherry, mountain ash and Norway maple will recover from a fairly hard prune. On the other hand, beech, birch and walnut dislike being pruned as large trees.

Branches that have been shortened will make new growth towards the end of the cut stem and in a short time will be as large as before and more bulky. Apply a surface feed to the root area in spring to help regenerate growth. Water the tree regularly in dry weather to help it recover.

1 Before you tackle an old tree, spend some time sizing up the job. Remove dead, diseased and crossing branches first. Cut them as close to the ground as possible: leaving stumps is not a good idea as they are prone to die back and become a source of disease.

Treating wounds

Traditionally wounds have been sealed with a proprietary paint in the same way as we cover a cut with a plaster. Recent research has shown the practice to be of little or no benefit, because the wound being covered is not sterile and the sealants are not air- or water-resistant. Call me old-fashioned if you will, but if there is a lot of canker disease about, I still slap on a wound paint which may prevent dangerous spores from entering through the wounds. Just allowing the cut to callus over naturally and seal the wound takes a long time. Other 'plasters', such as mastic sealants or household paint, may be tried, but I suggest you avoid bright pillar-box red or canary yellow!

2 Cut side branches where the collar joins the main branch or trunk.

ABOVE Bright young growths on willow. Coppiced every second year in spring to within 20cm (8in) of the ground, willow will respond with a mass of new growths with orange, purple or golden bark.

Coppicing & pollarding

The main difference between these two terms is the position where the pruning is carried out. Coppicing is done at ground level, while pollarding leaves a clear stem before cutting the tree close to its head. Both types of pruning result in a mass of vigorous, thin, whippy, year-old shoots ideal for basketwork, trellis, fencing and hurdles.

Trees grown for their coloured bark, such as willow, may be cut hard every second spring to encourage new growth that produces brighter colouring than the bark on older stems.

Coppicing trees such as the tree of heaven (*Ailanthus altissima*) and the foxglove tree (*Paulownia tomentosa*) results in enormous leaves that look dramatic in small gardens. The young foliage produced by coppiced *Eucalyptus gunnii* is a better shade of blue in the penny-shaped leaves that surround the stem. If you keep on doing it, eventually the tree will build up a mass of new shoots and some thinning will be necessary.

Propagation

There is something very satisfying about growing your own plants and even more so when the plant in question is a substantial tree. There are many methods of producing new plants, but not all are suited to every species of tree.

Sowing seed

When you see the ease with which nature germinates beech, oak, ash, alder, cypress and sycamore seed without the benefit of compost, propagator or Cheshunt compound to control fungal disease, you might think sowing seed is child's play. Sometimes it is. Many a garden remains shaded by a massive chestnut tree in the name of sentiment: 'He must have been all of three years old when he pushed it into the ground' is the usual explanation.

Some seeds require a period of cold before they germinate. Nature does it over the winter period for seeds in the ground. The alternative is to store the packets of seeds in the fridge for a few weeks. Others are even slower to get started, often taking a year before the seedlings emerge.

The easiest way to grow trees from seed is to sow them in trays or pots. Use a soil-based compost and label the containers as you sow. Make sure you use labels that will be legible for at least 12 months.

1 The depth of sowing in the compost depends on the size of the seed. Small seeds may be sown 1cm (½in) deep or on the surface; larger seeds should go deeper – in the case of the acorns of oak trees or the 'conkers' of horse chestnuts, up to 5cm (2in) deep. Sow thinly to give the seedlings the chance to grow in their own space and without their roots becoming tangled.

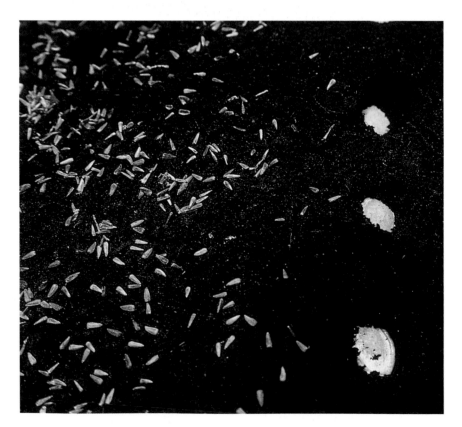

2 Cover the compost with a 1cm (½in) layer of washed grit or coarse sand. Stand the containers outside in a sheltered corner or under a hedge for the winter. Cover the pots with 1cm (½in) galvanised chicken mesh to prevent birds and mice eating the seed before it germinates.

3 Transplant the seedlings when they have produced true leaves – these appear after the first pair, which are the cotyledons or seed leaves.

5 Insert them in a soil-based compost with most of the stem covered, keeping the leaves just clear of the surface. Water immediately to settle the soil around the roots. Protect the seedlings from biting cold winds, which tend to scorch the foliage and dry out the compost.

4 Most seedlings are ready to be potted by the time they are 2-4cm (1-1½in) high. Take care when lifting them to prevent damage to the roots.

Taking cuttings

Male trees, such as some varieties of holly, obviously don't produce seed and have to be propagated by other means. Rooting small cuttings is a satisfactory method of propagating and works for both evergreen and deciduous trees. The resulting plants will be identical to the parent tree. Depending on the time of year and the firmness of the stems, the cuttings are referred to as softwood, semi-ripe wood or hardwood cuttings.

Variegated poplar (*Populus* x *candicans aurora*) is one of the easiest trees to propagate. Softwood cuttings taken in summer or hardwood cuttings taken in winter will soon become trees.

Softwood cuttings

Sophisticated equipment such as a heated propagator, soil-warming electric cable and a mist propagator will speed up the rooting process. Cuttings of some trees will be rooted within a few weeks.

At the other end of the sophistication scale, I thoroughly enjoy rooting softwood cuttings in a pot of compost covered with a polythene bag. This raises the humidity around the cuttings and prevents the leaves from transpiring and losing moisture before the roots form. Stand the pot in a well-lit window. Rooting will take a little longer than if you use the equipment mentioned above, but the resulting new young trees will be every bit as good. Pot the rooted cuttings singly in containers and plant out when 30cm (12in) high or grow on in larger containers.

Semi-ripe cuttings are taken later in the growing season, but before autumn. The stems should be quite firm and any soft extension growth should be cut off. These cuttings may be longer than softwood ones – 10-15cm (4-6in) and are slower to root. Treat them as for softwood cuttings.

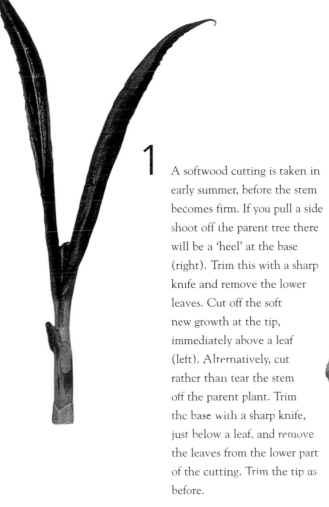

1 A softwood cutting is taken in early summer, before the stem becomes firm. If you pull a side shoot off the parent tree there will be a 'heel' at the base (right). Trim this with a sharp knife and remove the lower leaves. Cut off the soft new growth at the tip, immediately above a leaf (left). Alternatively, cut rather than tear the stem off the parent plant. Trim the base with a sharp knife, just below a leaf, and remove the leaves from the lower part of the cutting. Trim the tip as before.

2 A softwood cutting should be anything from 5cm (2in) to 10cm (4in) long. Dip the base of each cutting in hormone rooting powder or gel. This encourages the cutting to produce roots more quickly. It also contains a fungicide that reduces the risk of soil-borne fungal disease attacking the base of the cutting.

3 Insert the cuttings 2-4cm (1-2in) deep in a tray or pot of free-draining, gritty, soil-based compost.

Hardwood cuttings

The only requirement for hardwood cuttings is time: no compost, no rooting powder, no protection. A range of trees, shrubs and fruit bushes may be successfully rooted out of doors in 12 months.

1 Rooting hardwood cuttings is easy, needing no equipment other than a sharp knife. Take the cuttings in winter, using firm wood produced earlier that year.

4 Form a trench 15cm (6in) deep with vertical sides outside in a sheltered part of the garden. Line the base of the trench with coarse grit to improve drainage and insert the cuttings upright, 10cm (4in) apart.

2 Make each cutting 25-30cm (10-12in) long. Cut below the bottom bud or leaf.

3 At the top, make a sloping cut away from the leaf or bud. This allows rainwater to run away from the top bud rather than directly on to it. If dealing with an evergreen tree, remove the lower 15cm (6in) of foliage.

5 Firm the soil, make sure it is weed free and water well to settle the soil. Keep an eye on it and water again if it shows signs of drying out. The cuttings will be rooted after 12 months. They may then be dug up and planted out in their permanent position, or potted up to grow to a larger size before transplanting. Water again after planting out or potting up.

Root cuttings

Plants can be produced from some trees by taking root cuttings. This method is successful with paulownia and embothrium, for example.

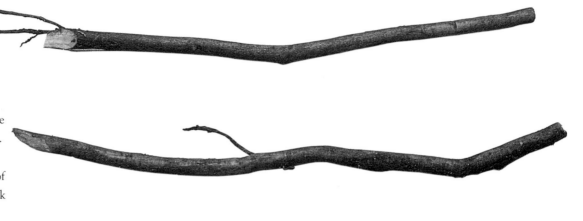

1 Cut healthy roots into 15cm (6in) lengths. Insert them upright in pots of soil-based compost with the top of the root at soil level. To avoid placing them upside-down, cut the end of the root closest to the trunk straight across and the other end at an angle.

Layering

Another slow but sure method is layering, where the lower branches of a tree that touch the ground are encouraged to root into the soil while still attached to the parent plant.

1 Check that the branch you intend to propagate can be bent to touch the ground along part of its stem. Loosen the soil and add grit and some well-rotted compost or leaf mould.

2 At the point where the branch is going to come in contact with the soil, use a sharp knife to make a sloping cut part way through the stem from the underside and wedge the wound open with a matchstick.

2   Water the pot and stand it in a cold frame. Eventually new roots will form and it will break into leaf.

Grafting

Grafting of trees is not really propagation. You start off with a tree but change it from a common species to a more ornamental variety. Grafting *Prunus sargentii*, with its beautiful autumn leaf colour, on to *Prunus avium*, the wild gean or cherry, still leaves you with one tree. The main benefit of a grafted tree is the vigour of the rootstock, which controls the size and speed of growth. In the case of fruit trees, for example, strong growing and dwarfing rootstocks are available.

3   Peg the branch firmly on each side of the weakened part.

4   Cover the branch with compost, placing a large stone on top to help retain moisture and secure the branch, which may also be staked to prevent movement during gales. After a year or two the branch will be well rooted and may be cut off from the parent tree. Take care to sever the branch on the side closest to the trunk of the parent. In winter, dig up the new rooted tree and plant it out.

Pests

In Britain mature trees are seldom subjected to serious damage from pests; sadly the same is not true of other parts of the world. But nor are we totally immune: young, newly planted trees are at risk and older trees may still succumb to diseases introduced by insects. A case in point is Dutch elm disease (see page 96). Pests are more easily controlled before they colonise a tree: the key is to examine plants frequently and know what you are looking for.

BORERS are serious pests in eastern parts of North America, where they attack many tree species, including crab apples and the black walnut. Larvae feed in the sapwood, forming tunnels up to 5cm (2in) long. The adults feed on the foliage.

Control: newly planted or stressed trees are most vulnerable. Maintain the tree's vigour by applying a spring feed. Remove damaged or diseased branches. Wrapping hessian or burlap around the main trunk of newly planted trees will prevent the female from laying eggs.

Borer

CHERRY BLACKFLY distorts and curls the young foliage at the tips of the branches of cherry trees. When the leaf is uncurled colonies of sap-sucking black aphids are visible.

Control: prune out and burn the infected leaves. Spray young trees with an aphid insecticide. In winter apply tar-oil wash to control the blackfly eggs. Japanese flowering cherries are seldom attacked.

Cherry blackfly

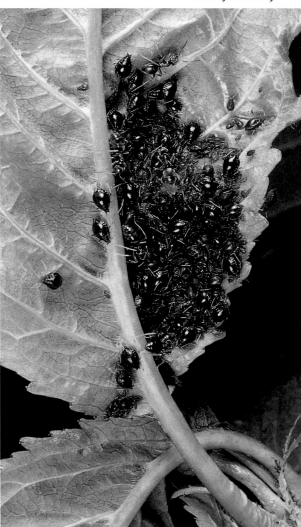

Greenfly

GREENFLY (APHIDS) spread virus disease on many plants from roses to beech trees. On some species of lime they excrete a sticky honeydew, causing a mess on the paintwork of cars parked underneath.

Control: it may be worth spraying young trees with an insecticide, but greenfly do little permanent damage to larger specimens. *Tilia* x *euchlora* is free of aphids.

Red spider mite

JAPANESE BEETLE is another mainly American pest. It attacks Norway maple, Japanese acer, horse chestnut, London plane, poplar, rowan and elm. The adult beetle is metallic green with orange-brown wing covers. Adults usually start to feed at the top of the plant and work their way downwards, chewing the tissue between the veins. Eggs are laid in the ground and the grubs spend most of their life in the soil.

Control: birds such as starlings eat the grubs. Or you can water the soil with a solution of milky spore disease, a bacteria that kills the grubs. It is sold under the brand names Japidemic or Doom. Adult beetles can be trapped with sweet-smelling bait.

RED SPIDER MITE causes yellowing of the needles and, if not treated, the defoliation of conifers such as the dwarf *Picea glauca* var. *albertiana* 'Conica' and *P. pungens* 'Koster', the blue spruce. From early summer the tiny pale green-yellow mites may be seen with the aid of a hand lens, but fine silk webbing over the foliage, towards the centre of the plant, is often the first visible sign. Different types of spider mite also attack fruit trees and greenhouse plants.

Control: spray using a systemic insecticide at weekly intervals for three to four weeks. Once you've got rid of an infestation, spraying regularly with water from a hose will help keep them under control.

WINTER MOTHS, in common with other moths, do no damage themselves. It's their caterpillars that are the problem. The moths emerge in winter, laying their eggs in the tree. Any deciduous trees are vulnerable, especially fruit trees. The male moth can fly, but the female has to crawl up the tree to lay her eggs. The caterpillars, which are green-yellow with pale stripes and appear in spring, feed on the foliage. They are easily recognised as they move by looping, having only a single pair of legs at either end of their body.

Control: fixing grease bands around the base of the trunk stops the female moth from climbing. To control caterpillars, spray the tree with a systemic insecticide as leaves appear in spring.

THE BROWN-TAIL MOTH CATERPILLAR causes dramatic-looking damage to hawthorn, cherry and other trees. The distinctive caterpillars are dark grey and hairy with red and white markings and two orange warts at the rear. They will strip a tree of foliage, covering the plant and themselves with a mass of fine, white silk webbing.

Control: prune out the overwintering larvae that hide in silk webs at the tips of shoots.

LARGER PESTS such as rabbits and hares may damage young trees by eating the bark, particularly when there isn't much other food around. Deer will eat young growths, as will horses, sheep, goats and cattle. Grey squirrels strip the bark and have, in recent years, become a serious pest to trees in Britain – if a ring of bark is removed from the main stem the plant will die. Tubular tree guards slipped over young saplings offer some protection and also save the tree from the careless use of strimmer and lawnmower. Site trees back from boundary fences to stop grazing animals from stretching over.

Winter moth caterpillar

Diseases

Even mature trees are not immune to disease and, in many cases, it is disease that shortens a tree's life.

ANTHRACNOSE can be due to one of several different fungi, each of which causes patches of discoloration on the tree. In severe cases, the tree may die. Plane anthracnose causes leaf buds to die in spring: the stem turns black and canker forms. In summer mature leaves are affected. Willow anthracnose affects the leaves, causing them to turn yellow, curl up and fall prematurely. Canker appears on the branches, which may die back.

Control: rake up and burn infected leaves. The Peking willow (*Salix babylonica* 'Pekinensis Pendula') is resistant to anthracnose.

ARMILLARIA, also known as honey or bootlace fungus, occurs as several different species, some of which are capable of killing the largest of trees in a season or two. Infected trees develop a creamy-white layer under the bark that smells of mushrooms. Black root-like organs

Anthracnose

called rhizomorphs, resembling bootlaces or tree roots, appear on the living or dead wood and spread about 1m (3ft) a year through the soil. In late summer and autumn, honey-coloured toadstools may appear around the base of infected trees. Birch, willow, cedar and cotoneaster are particularly susceptible to attack. Some trees, including beech, oak and yew, are less vulnerable.

Control: destroy infected plants as soon as possible and remove the surrounding soil.

BACTERIAL CANKER is a serious disease of *Prunus* species, especially cherry trees. The bark of affected trees is depressed, forming flattened patches. Where the bark is damaged, an amber-

Armillaria

Bacterial canker

coloured resin oozes out and solidifies. As the canker circles the branch, the leaves wither and die on the tree. Early infections show as small, yellow foliage. 'Shot hole effect' is caused when brown spots on the leaf die and fall out, leaving behind holes with brown edges.

Control: prune out infected branches in summer when the bacteria are less active. Spray with a copper-based fungicide in late summer and again in autumn. The disease is spread by wet, windy weather.

Dutch elm disease

CORAL SPOT DISEASE is capable of killing a tree and is particularly troublesome on acers, especially Japanese maples. Bright red or orange pustules may appear on decaying or dead branches at any time of the year. The spores are spread by rainfall, entering the tree through a wound or a dead snag left after pruning. Dieback occurs as the disease travels down the stem into the main trunk.

Control: check all trees carefully for dead snags and prune these and any infected stems back to healthy wood. Burn all infected prunings and dispose of rotting logs, old pea sticks and other debris that may harbour the pustules.

DUTCH ELM DISEASE, spread by elm bark beetle, is capable of wiping out all elms on a wide scale (as it did in Britain in the 1960s). The beetle forms tunnels under the bark and the adult carries the spores of the disease from tree to tree. Affected trees show severe wilting and yellowing of the foliage in the crown, especially during periods of dry weather. The leaves turn brown and die, and young shoots bend to form a 'shepherds' crook' shape. When cut, the stems of infected trees show circular brown staining of the current growths where the vascular system has been blocked.

There is no effective chemical treatment. Prune out and burn affected branches. Breeding for a resistant strain of elm continues.

FUNGAL CANKERS may be specific to one species of tree. Apple canker will attack all *Malus*, including crab apples. Poplar canker plays havoc with hedgerow poplars as well as the variegated

Coral spot disease

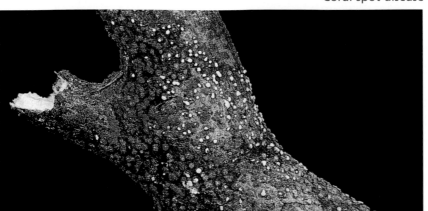

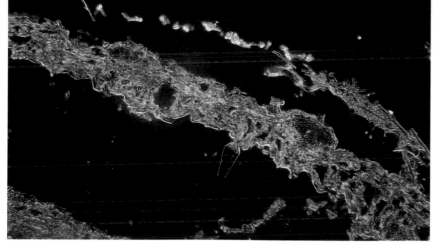

Phytophthora

garden form, *Populus* x *candicans* 'Aurora'. The disease is easier to spot in winter when there are no leaves to disguise the sunken patches of discoloured bark with surrounding swollen area.

Control: small areas of infection can be cut out, but once the canker circles the branch it will die.

PHYTOPHTHORA or COLLAR ROT is a soil- or water-borne disease that attacks the roots and the ground-level collars of trees. The fine feeder roots are killed and main roots are discoloured. The base of the tree also becomes discoloured under the bark. Most broad-leaved trees and conifers are susceptible: affected plants show symptoms of poor growth, leaf yellowing and dieback. In severe cases the plant will die.

There is no control other than removing and burning infected plants, and removing as much contaminated soil as possible.

SCAB is a common fungal disease that attacks the leaves and fruit of all the apple family (*Malus*), including ornamental crab apples. The spores overwinter on the ground on fallen leaves, and the disease is more evident during a wet, warm spring and early summer. Grey spots appear on foliage and dark brown spots form on the fruit. Badly infected fruit may crack and split open.

Control: rake up, vacuum up or burn with a flame gun all fallen leaves around the base of the tree.

TAR SPOT on sycamore rarely affects the vigour of the tree but the large, shiny, black spots are unsightly and are caused by a fungus.

There is no chemical control, but raking up and burning infected leaves in autumn will reduce the overwintering spores.

Fungal cankers

Scab

Tar spot

98

GARDENING WITH TREES

Trees are an integral part of the garden make-up. In planting terms, they may be thought of as large shrubs with the same dynamic mix of foliage, flowers and fruit. Even a single tree can influence the atmosphere and the physical appearance of its surrounding area. When a suitable species is given the correct conditions, its size may continue to control the site for generations; there is a future for trees long after our own existence. They should be planted for our enjoyment, but they also play an important role in screening the garden for privacy and shelter, and a tree-lined avenue makes an impressive welcome to any home while a single mature specimen planted in a lawn is always a statement to be heeded.

RIGHT A living screen providing shelter and privacy to a 'secret garden'. Early summer foliage and flowers are still fresh as a daisy.

BELOW Trees are adaptable and may be trimmed into shape. This apple tree (*Malus* 'Orléans Reinette') rewards your efforts with wonderful fruit and the espalier shape allows them all to get a sun tan.

Specimen trees for a lawn

LEFT With some trees the bark is spectacular, vying with the leaf, flower or fruit for attention. Here the cider gum (*Eucalyptus gunnii*) has peeled off its outer layer, revealing a patchwork of green, brown and cream. Quick-growing with aromatic, evergreen, sickle-shaped, blue-green foliage, it makes a bold specimen in a large garden.

BELOW *Amelanchier lamarckii* in its autumn glory. See page 10 for the spring blossom that is another reason for planting this fantastic tree.

There is no more spectacular sight than a mature tree, set in grass, without neighbouring plants to obscure its magnificence. As a solitary specimen it is not cramped and can spread to its full span. It doesn't have to be a large tree – its size should be in keeping with its surroundings. In addition to those listed here, small weeping trees such as the weeping purple beech (*Fagus sylvatica* 'Purpurea Pendula') can be eye-catching in a small lawn.

Ideal trees to plant as specimens include the yellow buckeye or American chestnut (*Aesculus flava*); the Indian bean tree (*Catalpa bignonioides*), which produces large trusses of white flowers with purple and yellow spots in summer, followed by long thin pods of seed; the evergreen Chilean fire bush (*Embothrium coccineum*), whose clusters of tubular scarlet flowers in late spring and early summer light up the dark green foliage; the cider gum (*Eucalyptus gunnii*), another evergreen, which may grow too large for many gardens but has startlingly blue-green juvenile foliage which is loved by flower arrangers; the bird cherry (*Prunus padus* 'Watereri'), whose hanging racemes of fragrant white flowers in late spring have a decidedly 'uncherry' look; and the evergreen *Eucryphia* x *nymansensis* 'Nymansay', which will impress the neighbours with its summer display of fragrant white flowers. And there is always *Amelanchier lamarckii*, gorgeous at any time of year.

Hedges and windbreaks

Trees may be used as hedges, the best example being the thousands of miles of hawthorn and blackthorn planted throughout Britain as field boundaries. Apart from marking the perimeter, they offer shade and shelter and a thorny deterrent to animals and trespassers. In the garden, beech, hornbeam and yew are commonly used as hedging plants and should be kept under control by twice-yearly clipping.

Trees to form a windbreak or dense hedge must be capable of growing in close proximity to their neighbours. Their branch structure needs to be dense with a network of strong laterals to filter the wind. Most are deciduous, but some evergreen trees, such as holly, can tolerate being planted close together.

Young bare-rooted trees (whips) are best planted in the late autumn when the ground is still warm. New roots will form and grow out into the ground, helping the plant become established before winter. As a general guide for windbreaks, the planting distance is 2m x 2m (6ft 6in x 6ft 6in) apart. The wider the belt of trees, the greater the area protected. A mixed planting, including evergreen and deciduous species with some autumn colour, will add interest to the shelter belt.

Ideal trees for windbreak hedges include the American hornbeam (*Carpinus caroliniana*), the English holly (*Ilex aquifolium*), the Antarctica beech (*Nothofagus antarctica*), the Lombardy poplar (*Populus nigra* 'Italica'), the Portuguese laurel (*Prunus lusitanica*) and the tupelo (*Nyssa sylvatica*), which is one of my favourites for autumn colour, with brilliant shades of

There is no better deciduous tree for pleaching than hornbeam (*Carpinus betulus*). Similar in habit to the common beech (*Fagus sylvatica*), it forms a tighter, more compact shape, with smaller leaves than lime and tolerates close clipping.

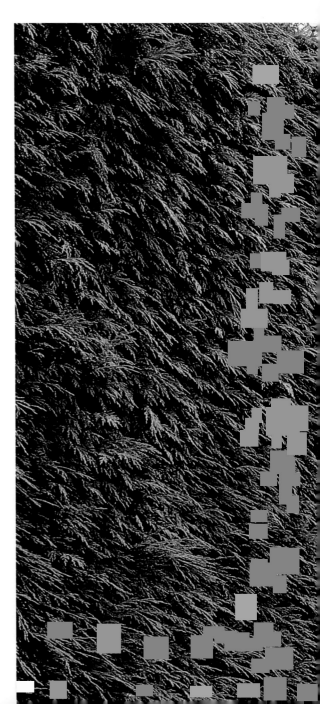

LEFT New foliage will soon clothe the hedge and arch of hornbeam, providing essential privacy.

BELOW *Chamaecyparis lawsoniana* makes a wonderful dense evergreen hedge. It is easily maintained up to 2m (6ft 6in) high.

yellow and gold turning to flaming red and finally a deep crimson. For single trees suitable for windy sites, see page 30.

Pleached hedges are a refinement whereby, every summer, the young, supple shoots are bent into the hedge, almost like weaving. The resulting hedge is strong and dense. Some trees, such as limes, which are very flexible, may be grown in a line as standards with a 2m (6ft 6in) high clear stem. Trees should be planted about 2-3m (6ft 6in-10ft) apart, then the young shoots trained on canes horizontally to meet the shoots of the next tree in the row, producing an attractive thin screen. Any lateral shoots below the desired height can also be tied to the horizontal cane, but try to bend them gently rather than breaking them.

One of the best examples I know of this is a row of pleached hornbeams to be found at Hidcote Manor in Gloucestershire. The perfect box-shaped hedges are on 1.2m (4ft) high bare trunks, and the line of hedge is clipped every summer.

Topiary

A prime example of tree shaping and the ongoing maintenance this requires is the art of topiary, in which trees are trained to form replicas of animals and birds, geometric shapes and pretty well anything else that takes the gardener's fancy. These are maintained through long hours of patience and toil. Topiary is usually done with evergreens such as holly. Evergreen conifers, especially yew, are ideal, forming a tight mass of foliage. Deciduous trees such as hawthorn may be used to good effect, showing the bare twig outline in winter.

It is essential that a dense framework is built up from early in the tree's life by frequent clipping to encourage the production of side shoots. Once the desired shape has been achieved, regular clipping – as frequent as once every two weeks during the growing season – is necessary to maintain a neat outline.

Espalier and fan-shaped trees are used for tree fruit such as apples, pears and peaches. Train the side shoots along wires on walls to form well-spaced branches which catch the sun and carry maximum fruit.

RIGHT Together, you and yew can let your imagination run riot.

BELOW A most unusual piece of topiary with a yellow dome of golden Irish yew (*Taxus baccata* 'Fastigiata Aureomarginata') growing above the dark green foliage of Irish yew (*Taxus baccata* 'Fastigiata').

Trees for avenues

A line of identical trees on either side of a drive leading up to the house is a wonderful sight and creates an impression of a bygone age. Even a row of trees lining a lane leading to a field is spectacular. It is usual to plant trees of the same species to create an avenue. Choose a tree suitable for the space available (i.e. one that won't grow too big for it) and ask the nursery or garden centre staff to select plants of similar height and spread. Plant both rows far enough back from the edges of the drive to prevent branches overhanging the roadway.

Plant the saplings in a line equidistant from the kerb. This way, if the drive sweeps, then the line of trees will match it. When staking, position the tree on the drive side of the stake to hide the support from passers-by. It's worth planting an extra matching tree at the same time somewhere else in the garden. Then if, for any reason, a tree dies, it can be replaced the following autumn with the spare one, without an obvious gap in the avenue.

Ideal trees for avenues include the Caucasian maple (*Acer cappadocicum* 'Aureum'); *Aesculus hippocastanum* 'Baumannii', a horse chestnut which has white double flowers in spring, but no conkers; the fern-leaved beech (*Fagus sylvatica* 'Aspleniifolia'); the evergreen *Lomatia ferruginea*; the unusual ornamental cherry (*Prunus* 'Kanzan') and the uncommon but gorgeous golden Dutch elm (*Ulmus* x *hollandica* 'Dampieri Aurea').

Trees for ground cover

A good ground-covering plant will prevent weeds from becoming a prob-lem. To this end, I do not believe plants have to hug the ground, forming a dense mat, to be weed suppressors. Evergreen trees, such as the evergreen oak *Quercus ilex*, with a leaf and branch canopy well above ground, are extremely effective in preventing weed growth. Even deciduous species, from dwarf acers to the enormous horse chestnut *Aesculus hippocastanum*, will deter weed growth.

In a mature woodland or forest, mosses and ferns are often the only sur-vivors on the forest floor. Years of decaying leaves result in a thick layer of

BELOW Evergreen oak is ground cover on a massive scale. Even weeds find life a trial in its dense shade.

RIGHT *Juniperus squamata* 'Holger' spreads quickly to form a mass of silver-blue growths which effectively smother germinating weeds.

leaf mould which, in a different situation, would be teeming with weeds.

The deep shade directly below a mature tree is inhospitable to most weeds. The mat of surface roots tends to leave the soil impoverished and dry to the point where weeds which have germinated will wither. The roots of some trees, such as pines, exude a toxin which prevents other plants from growing.

Grass generally and a lawn in particular are usually the first to die out under trees. The lawn sward becomes thin and patchy and weeds are reluctant to fill the gaps.

Carpeting under trees

That said, there are plants which enjoy a lightly shaded site where there is little or no direct sunlight. In a woodland situation, layers of leaves, shed annually by a deciduous tree, act as a mulch, suppressing weeds, keeping the soil temperature reasonably constant and improving soil structure. If they are allowed to remain they will be transported by worms down below the surface to raise the humus level in the soil.

In gardens, of course, we tend to rake the leaves up, so the soil around even a single tree will be impoverished as the roots spread far and wide in search of moisture and nutrients. The presence of a complex root system also makes the soil difficult to cultivate, and if you dig carelessly you will damage the roots. The best solution is gently to form planting holes between the roots and plant small container-grown plants.

Don't be in a hurry to carpet-plant. During its first year a newly planted tree will require attention and small plants close to the trunk will be a nuisance when watering, feeding and mulching. Checking the stake and loosening the ties as the tree grows will result in smaller plants being trampled.

In woodland bluebells often colonise the soil surface and they can be used to good effect in the garden, too. Wild garlic, winter aconites, violets and wood anemones also tolerate shade. *Anemone blanda* and *Cyclamen coum* will form sheets of colour as a result of self-seeding, spreading in areas of light shade where there is little competition from weeds. Bugle (*Ajuga*) and periwinkle (*Vinca*) are also effective ground-coverers, but they do tend to take over, so don't plant them anywhere that they will outcompete other cherished plants.

Pachysandra terminalis is a low-growing herbaceous perennial that prefers the cool shade of trees. Larger shrubs such as the spotted laurel (*Aucuba japonica* 'Crotonifolia') and butcher's broom (*Ruscus aculeatus*) will grow happily under trees which allow some light to penetrate. Ivy can make an attractive carpet, but in damp climates, as I know to my cost, it may become a weed and one which climbs every tree within its reach.

Old trees may be used as scaffolding to support climbers. Honeysuckle, clematis and rambling roses enjoy scrambling through large trees. Prepare a good planting pit close to the base of the tree and add moisture-retaining

compost and fertiliser. Encourage the plants to climb by giving them a 'leg up' on wire or plastic mesh.

It may be necessary to raise the head of some trees to allow ground-covering plants the space to grow. Lower branches may be trimmed or sawn off close to the main trunk. With smaller trees it may be sufficient to thin the existing framework of branches to let more light penetrate through to the ground beneath. Low, horizontal or drooping branches on specimen trees in the lawn may be removed for ease of access when cutting the grass.

Alternatively, removing the grass, where it is difficult to maintain around a tree, will prevent the base of the trunk being damaged by the mower. This circle of bare ground may be planted with ground-cover plants (see above) or bulbs and then mulched.

LEFT A 'carpet' of scilla bulbs flourishes under this *Magnolia sprengeri* 'Elongata'. Easy to grow, scilla will spread rapidly if you let it.

RIGHT Cyclamen love the cool shade offered by mature deciduous trees and will colonise large areas in a short time.

DIRECTORY OF TREES

QUERCUS ILEX
When space allows, the holm oak makes a magnificent evergreen specimen. The pendant yellow catkins (see page 185) and pretty acorns are worth a closer look.

You will feel a certain amount of relief and a lot of satisfaction when your short list of suitable trees emerges. Knowing that you have three, four or six species which all suit the site and conditions eases the mind. The final decision as to what to plant is usually down to personal choice and there is no substitute for going to see a tree growing. Where this is not possible it is an advantage to have an accurate, detailed description of what the mature specimen will look like, and that is what this section aims to provide. In my book, trees get extra brownie points for a combination of flower, berries, bark and leaf. Period of flowering and fragrance are worth noting. Food for birds is as important as colour of fruit, although growing a species whose fruit is devoured before it ripens seems pointless. Attractive winter bark and autumn leaf colour get double points for cheering me up on a dull day.

Acacia dealbata

MIMOSA, SILVER WATTLE

Mimosa forms a small evergreen tree that benefits from a sheltered sunny wall in all but the mildest of climates. The hairy, fern-like foliage is silvery green, 12.5cm (5in) long with up to 80 leaflets. Fragrant sprays of blossom appear in winter and spring as terminal racemes, made up of small, round, buttercup-yellow flowers, commonly known as 'florist's mimosa'. The seed pods are flat, blue-grey and 5cm (2in) long. Choose a suitable planting site as it dislikes being transplanted. Its country of origin is Australia, where it can reach 15m (50ft), but in most north European gardens 6m (20ft) is more usual with a spread of 5m (16ft).

Acacia rhetinodes

SILVER WATTLE

An evergreen tree with flattened leaf stalks called phyllodes, which take the place of leaves. They are grey-green, narrow and willow-like. Small lemon-yellow flowers are carried in clusters during summer. This acacia needs a sheltered site protected from frost and cold wind but it is one of the few that will tolerate an alkaline soil. When well sheltered it will grow to 6m (20ft) with a spread of 4m (13ft), but dislikes being hard pruned.

ACACIA DEALBATA
is quick-growing when sheltered from cold winds.

Acer

WITHOUT MAPLES, FORESTS AND GARDENS IN THE northern hemisphere would be a lot less interesting. The panorama of autumn colour in New England has to be seen during October, when no two plants appear to be exactly the same shade of red. Red maple (*Acer rubrum*) and sugar maple (*A. saccharum*) are indispensable for colour. (Maple syrup, for which I admit to having a weakness, is manufactured from the sap of the sugar maple.)

In Europe, sycamore (*A. pseudoplatanus*) and Norway maple (*A. platanoides*), with their red- and variegated-leaved offspring, add colour to parks, streets and gardens. Field maple (*A. campestre*) makes an excellent hedge in England, Ireland and Netherlands, as does Montpellier maple (*A. monspessulanum*) in southern Europe.

The maples of the East are in a class of their own. The Japanese maple (*A. palmatum*) is unsurpassed for planting in a small garden. The Chinese maple (*A. hersii*) has good red autumn colour and attractively striped bark.

All of the maples are happy growing in a moist, free-draining soil in a sunny or partially shaded site. They dislike a waterlogged soil. Only box elder (*A. negundo*) will thrive on a dry soil. Varieties of *A. palmatum* suffer from cold winds in spring when growth is commencing.

right
ACER PALMATUM 'FIREGLOW'
The Japanese maples are in a class of their own for leaf colour.

Acer cappadocicum 'Aureum'
CAUCASIAN MAPLE

There is a passage in the Bible where 'Paul went up to Cappadocicum'. This was a region in Asia Minor (modern Turkey) famous for its horses. The horses were traded to the Romans and, who knows, perhaps the trees were as well.

For my money this acer is a much superior plant to its other European rivals, the sycamore (A. *pseudoplatanus*) and the Norway maple (A. *platanoides*). It is more refined, with a pleasing shape when mature. Dome-shaped and growing to a height of 15m (50ft) with a spread of 10m (33ft), the tree has young foliage in a soft butter yellow in spring. The five- to seven-lobed leaves turn a glossy green in summer, finally reverting to a blaze of golden yellow in autumn. In spring the tree covers itself in small yellow flowers turning to clusters of 'keys' or seeds in early summer.

An easy tree to grow in all soil types except waterlogged conditions. It is tolerant of shade but enjoys a sunny site. The variety 'Rubrum' has spectacular blood-red young shoots in summer.

below
ACER DAVIDII SUBSP. GROSSERI
Typical winged seeds are attractive in late spring and early summer.

Acer davidii subsp. grosseri
SNAKE BARK MAPLE

Whenever I see this tree in winter, I want to give it a hug. The green-barked trunk and branches are boldly streaked with pure white stripes, hence its common name. This is one of the few trees that I am prepared to wash: if hosed down in autumn and rubbed with a piece of hessian sack it will be ready for its winter display. It is deciduous with mid-green triangular, shallow-lobed leaves.

In late autumn the tree lights up with bright orange-yellow foliage. Drooping pale yellow racemes of flowers appear in spring,

are grey-blue on the underside. In autumn they quickly turn to gold, red and scarlet. The yellow flowers hang in clusters followed by downy, winged seed. Germination of seed is poor, resulting in the paper bark being more expensive than most other acers. It will tolerate a range of soils including alkaline. Slow growing, it will eventually reach a height and spread of 9m (30ft).

Acer palmatum

JAPANESE MAPLE

There are other magnificent Eastern maples but the one every gardener considers as the Japanese maple is *Acer palmatum*. Shrub-sized but tree-shaped, it offers many choices of colour. The variety 'Shindeshojo' will slowly grow to 2m (6ft 6in) high and will have a spread equal to its height. The five- to seven-lobed leaves are, when they first emerge, a bright clear red. During summer they turn to a creamy-white and pink, speckled bright green, finally becoming

followed by long clusters of pale brown winged 'keys' or seeds.

It is quick growing in a well-drained, fertile soil. Avoid waterlogged soils which will cause the tips of shoots to die. Eventually it will make a large tree with a height and spread of 14m (46ft).

Acer griseum

PAPER BARK MAPLE

This is one of the most fascinating of all small deciduous trees. The old, rich brown bark peels like tattered and torn tissue paper, revealing the shining cinnamon-coloured young bark. The shedding of the outer layer occurs from an early age. The leaves are easily recognised by their three leaflets and

Acer pensylvanicum 'Erythrocladum'
MOOSEWOOD, STRIPED MAPLE

This is the only American striped-bark maple. It is deciduous and the 20cm (8in) leaves are pale green with three lobes pointing forward. In autumn they turn buttercup yellow.

The real beauty of this maple is the bright pink young shoots, which turn to red in winter. When mature, the bark turns to orange-red with white striations. The species itself, *A. pensylvanicum*, produces bright green, young stems vertically striped with white resembling chalk marks.

Mature trees are tall and sparse, more suitable for woodland or shelterbelt planting, with a height and spread of 10m (33ft) in the UK, 13m (43ft) in America. 'Erythrocladum' has a poor root system and benefits from support when young. It tolerates most soils but will not succeed in alkaline conditions.

flaming orange-red in autumn. When we have an 'Indian summer' with dry, warm wind and frost-free autumn days, this, my favourite maple, will hold its leaves and its colour almost into winter.

Plant it in a sheltered site in a fertile, well-drained soil with lots of leaf mould and compost.

All of the palmatum maples dislike cold winters. Mulch with a deep layer of bark or leaf mould to protect the root area from freezing. Spring frosts and cold winds will scorch young foliage if left unprotected. This tree gives great value for most of the year. It will suit the smallest of gardens and where there is only a balcony, plant it in a container for years of enjoyment.

above
ACER PALMATUM 'SHISHIO IMPROVED'
Sunlight playing on the leaves gives them a translucent look.

above right
ACER PALMATUM 'ATROPURPUREUM'
– a fine tree in old age.

Acer platanoides 'Crimson Sentry'
RED-LEAFED NORWAY MAPLE

A deciduous tree, this variety has an advantage over A. *platanoides* and its red-leaved variety 'Crimson King' in that it forms a narrowly columnar specimen rather than a large spreading tree. Quick growing, it will reach 11m (36ft) with a spread of 5m (16ft).

The leaves are red-purple and the clusters of yellow flowers appear before, or at the same time as, the new young foliage. Occasionally a branch will tend to grow sideways and, if not removed, will spoil the shape of the tree. None of the Norway maples is particular as to soil but they are short-lived in waterlogged conditions, preferring a well-drained site.

A. *platanoides* 'Drummondii' or variegated Norway maple is another deciduous variety which matures to a large size with a height and spread of 11m (36ft). As a young tree its foliage is most impressive: large five-lobed leaves open in spring with a yellow flush and quickly turn to mid-green with a creamy-white margin. Sadly this variety has a bad habit. It constantly tries to revert to its ancestral all-green leaf. Whole branches will revert and if they are not removed when young they will spoil the shape of the tree and eventually take over, growing more strongly than the variegated shoots. Check the tree at least twice a year when in leaf and remove the green-leaved shoots as close to the main trunk as possible.

Roots of Norway maples tend to spread over the surface of the ground and if planted as specimens in the lawn may cause problems when mowing.

Acer pseudoplatanus
VARIEGATED SYCAMORE

Acer pseudoplatanus is sometimes referred to as the English sycamore or the pseudo-plane tree. At one time it was thought to be the fig (*Ficus sycomorus*) that Zaccheus climbed in order to see Jesus over the heads of the crowd, hence its common name of sycamore.

It has been claimed that sycamore leaves on the track stop trains running and certainly the large five-lobed, dark green leaves are a nuisance in towns and close to housing. They block drains and gutters at the end of the season without the benefit of good autumn colour. The mustard-yellow, pendant flowers are abundant in spring, followed by winged seeds, which germinate readily and are classed by many as weeds. Its redeeming quality is that it is one of the toughest trees for coastal sites.

Acer rubrum 'Schlesingeri'

RED MAPLE, SCARLET MAPLE, SWAMP MAPLE

A round-headed, deciduous tree with 10cm (4in) long, three- to five-lobed, green leaves that turn a rich, dark red very early in the autumn. In late spring it produces erect clusters of tiny, bright red flowers. It will grow to 20m (66ft) in height with a spread of 8m (26ft).

Acer rufinerve 'Hatsuyuki'

SNAKE BARK MAPLE

Sometimes known as A. *rufinerve* 'Albolimbatum' this snake bark maple has arching branches striped with green and white. In late spring erect racemes of yellowish green flowers are followed in autumn by pale red-winged fruit. The deciduous 12.5cm (5in) long, three-lobed, leaves are mid-green with white mottling. It dislikes cold winds. At maturity it forms a tree 10m (33ft) high with a similar spread.

Acer tegmentosum

Although this tree is a native of north-east Asia, Americans love it. It is deciduous with three-lobed, dark green, 15cm (6in) long leaves that turn to golden yellow in autumn. Pendant bunches of greenish yellow flowers appear at the same

left
ACER RUBRUM 'SCHLESINGERI'
A clone of the Canadian maple which colours early in the autumn to a deep scarlet.

above
ACER RUFINERVE 'HATSUYUKI'
Even in autumn the silver shows through the brilliant red.

time as the new foliage. Its main attraction is the bright, green- and white-striped branches that seem to shimmer in the weak sunlight of winter. When the tree is young give the branches an autumn clean with a damp cloth. The show will be well worth the effort. This maple is slower growing than most others, forming a spreading tree with a height of 8m (26ft) and a spread of 9m (30ft). It is tolerant of most soil conditions but dislikes cold winds in spring.

Aesculus x carnea 'Briotii'

RED HORSE CHESTNUT

A deciduous tree, this is a favourite chestnut of mine and so much better in bloom than the paler pink flowering *A. x carnea*. The variety 'Briotii' originated in France and brings with it all the charm and grace of a true Parisian. The leaves are dark green with crinkly overlapping leaflets. Occasionally there is a hint of autumn colour. The deep red flowers, each with a yellow centre, appear in early summer and are carried in upright candle-like clusters, 25-30cm (10-12in) high. Occasionally smooth or slightly spiny conkers are produced.

It grows to be a large tree with a height of 18m (60ft) and a spread of 13m (43ft). If left unpruned and not grazed by animals, the branches will sweep down to ground level forming a dense spreading canopy. If large wart-like burrs appear on the main trunk leave them alone. They won't do any damage.

Aesculus flava

YELLOW BUCKEYE, SWEET BUCKEYE

A native of America, this beautiful, deciduous chestnut will grow well in all but the coldest areas of Britain. The dark green leaflets are finely toothed and of medium length. They colour well most autumns. The yellow flower candles appear in late spring and early summer and are 20cm (8in) tall and followed by smooth-skinned conkers. There is a pink-flowering form that grows wild in West Virginia. The yellow buckeye will grow in most situations but dislikes being transplanted as a large tree. It forms a conical tree 20m (66ft) high with a spread of 10m (33ft).

Aesculus hippocastanum

HORSE CHESTNUT

You may not have room for this magnificent, spreading, deciduous tree in your garden but you probably love it just the same. It has been grown in England since the time of Queen Elizabeth I and healthy trees in the county of Surrey have been dated to 1664.

The large, hand-shaped, mid-green leaves usually number five lobes but may have as many as nine. Those growing in Britain have better autumn colour than in

America. I have no idea why, I'm just glad that it is so. In my garden, the crinkly leaves turn a deep orange and are occasionally splashed with red.

In winter the shiny, mahogany buds of next year's leaves become sticky. The enormous candles of flowers appear in late spring and are white with a yellow centre that turns to red. In autumn 'conkers', beloved by boys and girls, fall to the ground, releasing their shiny brown seed.

The chestnut is a fast-growing tree ideal for parklands such as London's Hampton Court Palace and the boulevards of Paris. It will grow to 25m (80ft) and spread to 20m (66ft). It is happy in most soils but prefers a deep, moisture-retentive soil. The variety 'Baumannii' or the double-flowered horse chestnut has everything its parent has, plus one extra attribute: it is double flowered. The larger panicles of white 'candles' flower for a longer period and, being sterile, there are no 'conkers' to litter the ground and attract children. Like the rest of the chestnuts it is not fussy as to soil type. At maturity it forms a large open, spreading tree 25m (80ft) high and spreading to 15m (50ft).

Ailanthus altissima

TREE OF HEAVEN

The Chinese name for this tree translates as 'strong enough to reach heaven'. It is fast-growing with large, deciduous, pinnate leaves, each leaflet toothed at the base. The leaves are red-brown when they open, quickly becoming mid-green, and have an unpleasant smell when crushed. Be sure to grow female plants, as the male flowers stink. Pollen from male or female flowers may cause an allergic reaction. The large 30cm (12in) panicles of small green

left
AESCULUS HIPPOCASTANUM
This tree deserves its own space. Every child grows up recognising its big 'hand-shaped' leaf.

above
AESCULUS FLAVA
Our American cousins did the same to conkers as they did to the English language – they knocked off the rough bits!

flowers appear in summer, followed by winged seeds, which ripen to red.

The tree of heaven is prone to sucker at the base, quickly forming a thicket. It may be grown as a specimen in a small garden by pruning to within 30cm (12in) of the ground in spring and selecting one shoot to grow away. The resulting leaves are enormous and the plant will grow to 3m (10ft) in the first season. Left alone, a tree will grow to 25m (80ft) with a spread of 15m (50ft). It will prosper in the worst of soils.

In America it is unfortunately prone to fusarium disease.

Growing to 6m (20ft) with a spread of 4m (13ft), this dome-shaped deciduous tree has fern-like, mid-green leaves 45cm (18in) long. The leaflets are sickle shaped. Rounded clusters of fluffy pink flowers appear from summer until early autumn, followed by 12.5cm (5in) long seed pods.

Feeding young trees with a high potash liquid fertilizer in late summer will harden new growth and make it more resistant to frost damage. In spring, extremes of temperature may cause young shoots to die. The silk tree will grow best in an alkaline, well-drained soil that is not too well fertilized. A site sheltered from cold winds and in full sun will help to ripen the shoots and ensure a good show of flowers.

Alnus cordata

ITALIAN ALDER

Of the three alders generally grown, this has by far the most attractive foliage. The other two are the common English alder (*A. glutinosa*) and the grey alder (*A. incana*). Italian alder takes its common name from the fact that its timber was used for the piles that keep Venice afloat. Charcoal used in making gunpowder was originally produced from the timber of *A. cordata*.

The small, oval, finely toothed leaves of Italian alder are bright, glossy green and deciduous. Pendant brown-yellow male catkins 7.5cm (3in) long appear in late winter and early spring before the leaves. The egg-shaped, green, 2.5cm (1in) long cones appear in groups of three in summer, turning black in winter. Alders are the only broad-leaved plants to produce conifer-like cones.

Albizia julibrissin f. 'Rosea'

SILK TREE

With its origins in Iran, this member of the pea family is surprisingly hardy. The form 'Rose'a was introduced from Korea early last century and is sufficiently hardy to survive winter in most areas of Britain.

ALNUS CORDATA
The male catkins appear just as the leaves open.

Alders and rivers go together like strawberries and cream. They love moisture but the Italian alder will tolerate dry soil too. It is hardy and ideal as a windbreak. If pruning is necessary it is best done in late autumn or before the new year. Trees are fast growing, reaching 25m (80ft) with a spread of 7m (23ft).

Amelanchier 'Ballerina'

SNOWY MESPILUS

I love this tree. If I could only have one tree in my garden this would be it. It is deciduous yet manages to provide interest for most of the year. The star-shaped white flowers appear in long, arching racemes in the early spring ahead of, or at the same time as, the young foliage. The new leaves are bronze, turning to a glossy, mid-green in summer.

The fruit is sweet and juicy, red in summer, ripening to deep purple-black. It is good enough to justify netting the tree to prevent birds taking the lot. In autumn the foliage takes on a red-purple mantle lasting until the first frost.

The variety 'Ballerina' forms a tree 6m (20ft) high and spreading to 7m (23ft). It dislikes an alkaline soil, growing best in acid, wet, peat, and is a good companion for rhododendrons.

Amelanchier lamarckii

This species is often confused with A. *canadensis* and sold under that name. This is a shame since the true A. *canadensis* is a wild, suckering shrub in North America and certainly not ideal for growing in the garden. It makes a larger tree than 'Ballerina' with the same light framework of branches. The young foliage opens as a

AMELANCHIER LAMARCKII
The veins remain a pale green-yellow, giving each leaf a hand-painted look.

silky bronze-pink in early spring quickly turning dark green, before putting on a brilliant autumn display of orange and red. The veins remain pale green-yellow, giving each leaf a hand-painted look. The pure white star-shaped flowers hang in pendant clusters, up to 10cm (4 in) long, in early spring at the same time as the leaves unfurl. Prolific in flower, it makes a

spectacular display for 8-10 days. The purple-black fruit are small with good flavour when cooked. Totally hardy it grows best in a moist, fertile, well-drained, acid site to a height of 10m (33ft) with a spread of 11m (36ft).

Arbutus menziesii
MADROÑE, MADROÑA

This is the stunning madroña of California, growing wild from there to British Columbia. Evergreen, glossy, dark green foliage, glaucous on the underside, contrasts with the smooth, cinnamon-red bark. Seeing this tree, with its bark and foliage lit by a pale winter sun, makes you realise how important evergreens are in the garden.

Unlike the strawberry tree, this arbutus flowers in early summer with large, conspicuous, upright panicles of white, urn-shaped blooms. The rough-skinned fruits from the previous year's flowers appear in early autumn. They are usually yellow or orange and occasionally red. The Portuguese use them to distil a local spirit. Like Irish poteen, it is illegal to make but doesn't taste as good, I'm told.

Again it differs from the strawberry tree in needing an acid soil. It is not as hardy as A. *unedo* and in Britain succeeds best in a sheltered site in full sun, protected from cold winds, where it will grow slowly to a height and spread of 13m (43ft).

Arbutus unedo
KILLARNEY STRAWBERRY TREE

A native of south-west Ireland and the Mediterranean area, the strawberry tree is one of my favourite evergreen trees. The 'strawberries' are edible but the species name *unedo* means 'I eat one only' – a good description since they taste vile.

The dark green, glossy leaves are slightly toothed. The bark is a wonderful shade of deep chestnut brown with a hint of red.

ARBUTUS UNEDO
Until it reddens (see page 29), the 'strawberry' fruit looks decidedly tropical.

Old specimen trees are gnarled and twisted with shredding bark. For a better view of the main stems the head of the tree may be lifted by removing the lower branches; this is best done in spring. The white, lily-of-the-valley like flowers with a pink tint hang in clusters in the autumn at the same time as the fruit from the previous year's flowers. The fruits are red and rough skinned, almost warty.

A. *unedo* is the hardiest species and will thrive in many areas in Britain. Unlike most ericaceous plants it is tolerant of an alkaline soil and it will withstand salt-laden winds in maritime sites. A strawberry tree will grow more quickly if transplanted as a small container-grown plant, to reach a height and spread of 7m (23ft).

Azara microphylla 'Variegata'

Originating in Chile and Argentina, this tree will enjoy the protection of a sunny wall. It is a charming evergreen with small very dark green leaves, 2.5 cm (1in) long; each leaf has a margin of cream forming a herring-bone pattern on the pendant stems. The small, vanilla-scented, greenish-yellow flowers appear in late winter and early spring on the undersides of the branches. The flowers are mostly composed of stamens without petals. The tree prefers a moist, fertile, free-draining soil with added compost. It is reasonably hardy, but young growths will suffer from a spring frost or a cold wind. It is slow-growing, but will eventually reach 8m (26ft) with a spread of 4m (13ft).

AZARA MICROPHYLLA 'VARIEGATA'
The level of variegation varies from plant to plant. Select a tree with broadly margined leaves.

Betula

BETULA ALBO-SINENSIS
Peeling bark is just one of the many attributes of birch trees.

BIRCH TREES, AGAINST ALL THE ODDS, survived the last Ice Age. They have the ability to endure the most awful climatic conditions: the dwarf *Betula nana* is to be found growing within the Arctic Circle. The birch enjoys the wind in its hair and loves to have its feet close to, if not in, water. The poet Samuel Taylor Coleridge referred to it as 'the lady of the woods' and its elegant poise and slim, pale, graceful beauty suggest femininity. The branch structure tends to be open and thin, with the main stems quickly tapering to whippy twigs. The small leaves are well spaced, giving the tree a light, airy feel and allowing daylight through to the lawn or woodland floor. In winter the mass of twiggy stems filters strong winds, reducing their force.

In spring the golden-brown male catkins, which are longer than the female but carried on the same tree, dangle like lamb's tails. In autumn, leaves turn honey-yellow and brown before carpeting the ground.

The real beauty of the birch is its bark. Mature trees, with every branch coloured, stand out like ribbons in the dullest garden. Despite its common name, the silver birch is seldom that – most 'silver' birch are grey or brown barked. Instead, the colours on my list include gleaming white *B. papyrifera* and *B. jacquemontii*, pink-barked *B. albo-sinensis*, pinky-cream of *B. costata*, brown-black and rough-barked *B. nigra* and the amber bark of the tall-growing American *B. alleghaniensis*.

Birch are at home in heathland, moors, bog, mountain and woodland. *Betula pendula*, in particular, will grow on acid and alkaline soil, although in America it is prone to the birch borer insect pest, which may kill the tree.

Trees 'bleed' if branches are cut as the sap is rising in spring. Pruning to lift the head of the tree to display the bark should be carried out between early autumn and early winter.

Betula ermanii 'Grayswood Hill'
ERMAN'S BIRCH

This tall, quick-growing Russian birch will reach 20m (66ft) with a spread of 12m (40ft). The shoots are rough and warty with 10cm (4in) long, dark green leaves that turn yellow in autumn. The pendulous male catkins are yellow-brown and 10cm (4in) long in spring.

Bark on the main trunk is pink-white and covered in pale brown pores known as lenticels. It peels in tissue-thin layers. The

right
BETULA NIGRA
Plant birch for dappled shade on a hot summer's day.

below
BETULA ERMANII 'GRAYSWOOD HILL'
Yellow-brown male catkins and white bark are a spring treat in the garden.

young branches are orange-brown.

The species *B. costata*, also from north Asia, is quite rare. Most trees so labelled turn out to be *B. ermanii* 'Grayswood Hill'. The real thing will quickly grow to 30m (100ft) with pure white bark, in a sunny situation in any soil other than waterlogged.

Betula nigra
RIVER BIRCH, BLACK BIRCH

This fast-growing native of North America differs from most other birch with its cracked and peeling dark-brown mature bark instead of the usual smooth, polished pale surface.

The diamond-shaped, 7.5cm (3in) long, dark green leaves are glaucous on the underside. Overnight, in early autumn, the foliage turns deep yellow. Male catkins appear in early spring at the same time as the leaves and are 8cm (3in) long and pendulous. As the common name suggests, this is the birch to plant beside a lake or river where its roots may remain moist.

The variety 'Heritage' is an improvement with creamy-brown bark and glossy leaves. It is also a more vigorous form and was found as a seedling in America.

Betula pendula
SILVER BIRCH

This is the birch usually given to mark a silver wedding anniversary, yet, in truth, its bark is a chalky-grey, becoming black-brown and deeply cracked as the tree ages. The branch system is thin and pendulous with rough, warty shoots. Mid-green, diamond-shaped leaves, 6cm (2.5in) long turn yellow in autumn. Silver birch will quickly grow to 25m (80ft) with a spread of 10m (33ft). It prefers an acid soil but will succeed on a limy site.

There are some excellent varieties of *B. pendula*, including 'Laciniata' with deeply cut leaves. 'Purpurea' has purple-tinted bark and deep brown-purple leaves, growing to 10m (33ft) with a narrow spread of 3m (10ft). Watch out for and avoid 'Golden Cloud'. It is a recent introduction with pale, sickly yellow foliage which scorches in strong sunlight. When planted in shade it almost always reverts to pale green. The variety 'Youngii' or Young's weeping birch is a good tree for the smaller garden. It will eventually reach 8m (26ft) with largely a one-sided spread of 4m (13ft). When mature it forms a mushroom-shaped head, the top branch at right angles to the main stem. The tree is densely twiggy and the diamond-shaped leaves are deeply toothed, turning bright yellow in autumn.

After a fall of snow the tree almost disappears, camouflaged as a snow drift. It will succeed best in a fertile, moisture-retentive, well-drained soil in a sunny site.

above

BETULA PENDULA
The longer male catkins hang down. Female catkins are smaller and eventually become pendulous.

right

BETULA UTILIS VAR. JACQUEMONTII
My favourite birch. In my garden the green would be washed off the main branches every autumn.

Betula utilis var. jacquemontii
HIMALAYAN BIRCH

I love this tree. Every winter I wash the trunk and main branches with clean water and a cloth to remove any dirt and green algae. As a result, the bark is pure white and, in winter when bare, the branches stand starkly white against an overcast sky.

A deciduous tree with an open habit of growth, all the Himalayan birch's branches tend to be upright. The oblong, dark green, doubly toothed leaves, up to

12.5cm (5in) long, turn yellow in the autumn. Pale brown 12.5cm (5in) long male catkins are produced in early spring, releasing clouds of pollen in the slightest breeze.

Betula utilis var. *jacquemontii* 'Grayswood Ghost' has shiny foliage and brilliant white bark.

These trees grow best in a well-drained soil in full sun or partial shade, to a height of 18m (60ft) with a spread of 10m (33ft).

Broussonetia papyrifera
PAPER MULBERRY

A round-headed deciduous tree which will manage not only to survive, but also to grow happily in the poorest of soils. The leaves are dull green and rough textured on the upper surface, woolly on the underside. Occasionally they are oval-shaped but more often they are deeply lobed and attractive, like those of their relative, the fig. Male and female flowers are carried on separate plants. The male flowers appear, in late spring, as pendant 7.5cm (3in) long catkins with pale yellow anthers. The ball-shaped female flowers are 2.5cm (1in) across with purple stamens and are followed, in autumn, by sweet, edible, orange-red fruits like mulberries. In China and Japan the bark is still used to make top-quality writing paper. It is soaked, smoothed out flat and brushed over with rice paste. The Polynesians use it to make a type of cloth.

The paper mulberry tends to sucker: remove them before they quickly form a thicket. It prefers a well-drained soil in a sunny situation, growing to a height and spread of 8m (26ft).

Camellia reticulata 'Captain Rawes'

This variety was the first C. *reticulata* to be introduced to Britain from western China in 1820 by plant hunter Robert Fortune. Most camellias are best treated as shrubs but, in the right situation, 'Captain Rawes' will outgrow many trees. It is an evergreen, with leathery, dull, dark green leaves. The flowers appear in mid to late spring and are semi-double, pink-red, up to 15cm (6 in) across. This species is less hardy than the more commonly grown C. *japonica*. It requires a favoured site against

below
CAMELLIA RETICULATA 'CAPTAIN RAWES'
Grown in a sheltered site, the blooms can be up to 15cm (6in) across.

right
CARPINUS BETULUS
In autumn the leaves turn from green to lemon and orange.

a sunny wall or a mild, virtually frost-free garden. It prefers a slightly acid, free-draining soil. Camellias produce lots of surface roots and must not be planted deeply. A surface mulch applied every year will keep the roots cool.

The flowering buds form in late summer. Any shortage of moisture at this time may result in bud drop later on, where the fat flower buds drop prematurely before they can open. 'Captain Rawes' is usually propagated by grafting, making it more expensive to buy. It will grow to a height of 10m (33ft) with a spread of 5m (16ft).

Caragana aborescens 'Pendula'
WEEPING PEA TREE

This bushy deciduous tree produces stiff pendant shoots. It is one of the most easily grown trees, tolerating all types of soil and weather conditions. It originates from Siberia and North China, which explains why it doesn't mind what type of weather

we throw at it. The main stems carry vicious thorns and pale green pinnate leaves. Clusters of pale yellow flowers are produced in late spring, followed in the autumn by long, thin, pale brown pea-like seed pods. The species *C. arborescens* is ideally suited as a tough windbreak, mixing well with hawthorn to form an impenetrable barrier. The weeping form, however, is usually top grafted, resulting in a permanently thin stem and a weakness where the head forms. Stake the tree with one tie below the graft and another holding the head secure. It reaches a height of 2m (6ft 6in) with a spread of 1.5m (5ft).

Carpinus betulus

HORNBEAM

Frequently mistaken for beech, the common hornbeam is, in my opinion, a far better tree. The common name dates from the 12th century, when it was called the 'horny' tree to describe the hardness of the timber. It was also referred to as 'iron-wood' and before iron became cheap, the timber was used to make cogs and load-bearing axles. It was used for milk churns and today some of the working parts of pianos are still made from hornbeam.

Unlike the beech the mature bark is deeply fissured and the leaves are saw-edged. Like the beech it is a superb plant for hedging and pleaching.

The variety 'Columnaris' forms a narrow, upright deciduous tree with mid-green leaves that colour to gold and orange in autumn. In spring, it produces yellow male catkins and longer, green female catkins, followed in autumn by hanging clusters or chains of three-winged nuts. If they are not blown away

by autumn winds, they remain long after the leaves have fallen.

Hornbeam will tolerate most soil conditions and is totally hardy. As the tree ages it loses its fastigiate habit, broadening out to form a tree 10m (33ft) high with a spread of 5m (16ft). It can be transplanted as a large specimen. The variety 'Fastigata' matures as a larger and broader tree.

Carpinus carolinia

AMERICAN HORNBEAM, BLUE BEECH

If anything, the timber of this species of hornbeam is even tougher. It forms a small, spreading, deciduous tree with drooping branches. The leaves are a shiny, pale blue-green colouring to autumn shades of yellow, orange and red. The bark on mature trees is smooth grey. The female catkins are green, up to 10cm (4 in) long,

followed by pendant clusters of green, winged nuts which turn golden-brown.

It is ideal as a windbreak and it is tolerant of very hard pruning. It will grow in most soils but cannot cope with waterlogged conditions. It grows to a height of 10m (33ft) with a spread of 12m (40ft).

Carya ovata

SHAGBARK HICKORY

If you garden you will know that hickory is the very best timber for the handles and shafts of your tools. In America it is common enough to be used for barbecue fuel.

You can recognise this hickory by its bark, which is how it gets its common name. After 25 years the dull grey tattered and torn bark twists away from the trunk in long strips. Unlike other hickories, the

shagbark has five (rather than seven) deciduous leaflets, the terminal three being much larger than the bottom two.

It is a valuable nut-producing tree in America but is less reliable in northern Europe, except after a long, hot summer. The leaves colour to a brilliant yellow in autumn but quickly drop when the evenings turn cool. In late spring the hairy, greenish-yellow male catkins and three-pronged, green female catkins are produced on the same tree. These are followed by white pecan nuts, quartered inside a hard shell.

The tree prefers a rich, deep, well-drained soil but, like all the hickories and their cousin the walnut, it quickly forms a tap root that dislikes disturbance. For this reason it should be transplanted only as a small pot-grown plant. The shagbark will grow to 25m (80ft) with a spread of 12m (40ft).

left above
CARYA OVATA
You may not get a crop of nuts but the foliage is handsome and turns butter-yellow in autumn.

left below
CASTANEA SATIVA
The Spanish chestnut is yet another tree worth growing for its striking leaves.

below
CATALPA BIGNONIOIDES
Large tree, large leaves and large 'candles' of flowers.

is used for cleft stakes for chestnut fencing. The 20cm (8in) long, toothed leaves are shiny and dark green. In spring the tree is covered with long creamy catkins noted for their unpleasant smell. In autumn edible nuts are produced inside prickly green shells. Each case contains two to three nuts. The variety 'Marron de Lyon' produces the sweetest-tasting fruit. Hot, roasted chestnuts bring back childhood memories but a long, hot summer is required for a good crop. The chestnut prefers an open, free-draining acid soil. It will make a large tree 30m (100ft) high with a spread of 15m (50ft).

Catalpa bignonioides

INDIAN BEAN TREE

In this case the Indian refers to Native American Indians. *Catalpa* is an Indian rather than a Latin word, meaning 'winged

Castanea sativa

SPANISH CHESTNUT, SWEET CHESTNUT

Although not a native species, this tree has been grown in Britain since Roman times and may have been introduced by them. Unfortunately, in North America, the Spanish chestnut has been wiped out by chestnut bark blight and the Chinese chestnut *C. mollissima* is grown in its place. The native American chestnut, *C. dentata*, has also been lost to disease, which is a shame since this was Longfellow's 'spreading chestnut tree' under which the 'village smithy stood'.

Sweet chestnut is a deciduous tree which, in maturity, has an enormous girth and its smooth bark becomes deeply cracked with spiralling patterns. Its timber

will also shred and destroy the large, soft foliage. Pollarding the tree every year to within 30cm (12in) of the ground results in strong, 3m (10ft) tall stems with enormous leaves. By pollarding, the Indian bean tree may be planted in a confined space. It prefers a well-drained soil in full sun with shelter from strong, cold winds. It will grow to a height of 14m (46ft) with a similar spread.

The variety 'Aurea' or golden-leaved bean tree is breathtaking in summer. The large golden, velvety leaves are striking in sunlight. I would love to have the space and the audacity to plant a copse of 'Aurea'. On a sunny day it would look like the pot of gold at the end of the rainbow. The flowers and seed pods are as described for C. *bignonioides* but it is more prone to damage by a late spring frost. It is smaller, growing to a height and spread of 10m (33ft).

Celtis occidentalis

NETTLE TREE, HACKBERRY

This deciduous tree is easily recognised by its rugged, knobbly, corky bark. The sharply toothed leaves are shiny mid-green on the upper surface, pale green on the underside.

In spring small green male flowers are produced at the tips of twigs. At the same time female flowers appear at the leaf axils. In autumn fleshy, yellow, red or purple, edible fruit are produced. The nettle tree dislikes waterlogged soil, as the roots go deep, resulting in a tree which never suffers from drought. In cooler climates it tends to branch, forming a cluttered shape. It also has a habit of forming 'witches' brooms', great clusters of twigs that may be the result of a fungus

head' and referring to the flower shape. As a deciduous tree it matures to a wonderful spreading specimen for a large lawn. The bold, heart-shaped leaves unfold purple, turning pale green and downy. By mid summer they are glossy green with an unpleasant smell if crushed. On mature trees the summer flowers are spectacular, forming pyramidal trusses; each white, bell-shaped flower is frilled at the edge with purple and yellow spots. These are followed, in autumn, by 40cm (16in) long, hanging bean-like pods.

The branches are pithy and brittle, subject to damage in strong winds, which

CELTIS OCCIDENTALIS
Beautiful in bark and leaf, the tree's autumn fruits are edible.

horizontal. The leaves are heart-shaped at the base and bronze when young; in summer they become blue-green on the upper surface, pale green on the underside. In autumn the foliage colours beautifully with brilliant shades of gold, orange and red. When the leaves fall they give off the aroma of burnt sugar. It's like being in a fudge factory. Occasionally single leaves will be produced on the older wood – in autumn these look just like splashes of paint on the bark.

Katsura will grow on an alkaline site but, for the best leaf colour, plant it in an acid soil. It will tolerate a dry soil but it prefers it to be deep, moist and fertile. It dislikes cold winds and early spring frosts, which cause serious damage to the young shoots. There is a smaller uncommon species, *C. magnificum*, with larger, longer leaves and growing to 9m (30ft) with a spread of 7m (23ft).

Cercis siliquastrum
JUDAS TREE

The story persists that this is the tree from which Judas Iscariot hung himself. It is a pity to spoil a good legend but in France the tree is named *l'arbre de Judée*, translating as 'the tree from Judaea'. It is deciduous, with a height and spread of 10m (33ft). The heart-shaped leaves are bronze when young, turning glaucous, blue-green and finally clear yellow in autumn. The new shoots form a zig-zag, changing direction at each leaf stalk.

Tiny purple-pink flowers cover the tree before, and at the same time as, the foliage in late spring. The flowers have the unusual habit of also appearing in clusters directly from the bark of the oldest branches. They are followed by

attack or damage from mites. These constantly shed twigs and litter the ground below. The variety 'Magnifica' is immune to this disfiguration. In a sheltered site it will grow to 20m (66ft) with a spread of 13m (43ft).

Cercidiphyllum japonicum
KATSURA TREE

This deciduous, fast-growing tree will grow to 20m (66ft) with a spread of 15m (50ft). It usually forks close to ground level, forming a pyramidal shape. The older branches tend to droop, becoming

CERCIDIPHYLLUM JAPONICUM runs through practically the full spectrum of colours in the course of a year. Here it is beginning to turn from summer green to autumn yellow. When the leaves eventually fall the surrounding area will smell like a fudge factory.

purple seed pods. The variety 'Alba' is white flowering.

Cold winds and frost in spring may kill a young plant. Feed high potash liquid feeds in autumn to harden new growth. Plant small container-grown trees as they dislike transplanting. In America the species *C. canadensis* (eastern redbud) is a better choice as it is more hardy. The variety *C. c.* 'Forest Pansy' has deep purple leaves.

CERCIS SILIQUASTRUM
has the ability to produce flowers directly from the bark of old branches where there are no leaves.

Chionanthus virginicus
AMERICAN FRINGE TREE

Planted for effect, this slow-growing, deciduous tree is spectacular in early summer. The 20cm (8in) long leaves appear in late spring. They are bright, glossy green on the surface, slightly downy on the underside and turn toffee-yellow in autumn. The flowers, hanging in loose panicles up to 20cm (8in) long, appear to have been put through a shredder. Each flower has four thin, pure white petals and is slightly fragrant. On mature trees enormous quantities of flowers cover the tree. Male and female flowers are carried on separate plants and female trees bear small, fleshy, inedible, blue-black egg-shaped fruits with a single seed.

The fringe tree loves a well-drained, acid soil in full sun. In Britain it will only fruit after a long, hot summer and won't grow much higher than 4m (13ft) with a spread of 3m (10ft). In North America it grows to 9m (30ft). Removing the lower branches gives it a more tree-like appearance.

Cladrastis lutea
YELLOW-WOOD

A medium-sized, rounded, deciduous tree with pale green pinnate leaves that turn bright yellow in late autumn. It grows to 12m (40ft) with a spread of at least 9m (30ft). The pendant, fragrant panicles of white flowers appear in late spring and early summer, resembling wisteria flowers. These are followed by long streamers of dark brown seed pods, which hang well into winter.

When first cut the wood is yellow, hence the common name. The stems are brittle, suffering damage in strong winds.

left
CLADRASTIS LUTEA
As the new leaves emerge they look fragile, but soon clothe the tree, turning yellow in autumn.

blue-black berries. The young foliage tends to suffer from cold, biting winds in spring. It dislikes a waterlogged site but is tolerant of an alkaline soil. Smaller growing than the green-leaved C. *controversa*, its maximum height and spread is 7m (23ft).

If the leader of the tree is damaged it will grow into a rounded, many branched, shrubby specimen. When it is necessary to shape it, prune in late summer to prevent bleeding. It prefers a deep, loamy, fertile, acid soil: on a chalk soil it has a short life.

Cornus controversa 'Variegata'
WEDDING CAKE TREE

A cornus with attitude. When in leaf, a mature specimen of this tree will stop you in your tracks. It is a plant of rare beauty that refuses to conform to normal tree shape. The branches stretch out horizontally, forming tiers sufficiently far apart to allow light and shade to play on the lower branches – no wedding cake ever had as many layers.

The deciduous 15cm (6in) long, oval leaves are glossy green, margined with creamy-white or yellow. In early summer mature trees produce masses of small, pure white flowers in flat clusters, followed by

CORYLUS AVELLANA (see next page) is worth growing for the attractive nuts, which have the bonus of being delicious.

Corylus avellana

HAZEL

A large shrub or small tree with deciduous mid-green leaves. The bright yellow, male, pendulous catkins appear in winter and early spring, releasing clouds of sulphur-yellow pollen. Edible hazel nuts, in a hard shell, ripen in autumn.

Hazel prefers a well-drained alkaline soil in sun or light shade. It will grow to 5m (16ft) high with a similar spread.

Cotoneaster 'Cornubia'

Most species of cotoneaster are shrubs and a proportion of those are low-growing ground-hugging plants. 'Cornubia' is in a league of its own, prepared to stand up and rightly claim to be a tree. Generally semi-evergreen it may, without damage, lose all its leaves when temperatures stay low for a long period. If one branch is selected as a leader and the remainder removed, 'Cornubia' will quickly form a tree with a good-sized trunk.

The 14cm (6in) smooth, narrow, dark green leaves are slightly downy on the underside. Small white flowers, which attract bees in great numbers, appear in early summer followed by masses of clustered large, bright, red fruit. The branches arch downwards, the curve becoming more pronounced as the fruit swells. Our feathered friends will ignore the fruit until they consider it to be ready. At that stage the tree becomes alive with birds, whose weight may bend the branches. Hours later, every berry has disappeared.

Its speed of growth makes 'Cornubia' an ideal dot plant in a windbreak, brightening the dullest planting scheme. It will grow on most soils but prefers a sunny site. It quickly reaches a height of 6m (20ft) with a similar spread.

Cotoneaster 'Hybridus Pendulus'

WEEPING COTONEASTER

When grown as a standard this semi-evergreen forms a small tree ideal for a container. The 7.5cm (3in) long, glossy, dark green leaves form a dense canopy on a framework of weeping branches. Clusters of small, white flowers appear in early summer. In autumn the branches are laden with brilliant, bright red berries. If unpruned the branches will continue to grow horizontally along the soil or hard surface. Where space permits, allowing the berried branches to carpet the edge of a patio can introduce a softening effect. It will grow happily in most situations with the exception of wet, poorly drained soil.

As it matures, the trunk remains thin but the tree develops a bulky head, so it

left
CORYLUS AVELLANA
Clouds of pollen appear when the male
catkins are disturbed in a breeze.

below
CRATAEGUS LAEVIGATA 'PAUL'S SCARLET'
– after the mass of pink flowers (see
page 30), the 'haws' are scarce and small.

It may be planted to form a dense hedge,
ideal for livestock control. Most soils are
suitable but it will succeed best on an
alkaline soil, growing to 6m (20ft) with a
spread of 5m (16ft). The deciduous, glossy,
dark green leaves are deeply lobed and
diamond-shaped with a downy grey
underside. In summer the dense clusters of
up to 12 white flowers with red anthers are
followed by large, orange-red fruit in
autumn. Occasionally the fruit are red,
flushed with yellow.

Crataegus laevigata 'Paul's Scarlet'

RED HAWTHORN, MAY TREE, ENGLISH HAWTHORN

In England it is always hoped that the
hawthorn is in flower for May Day, the
first Monday in May and an important
event in every socialist's calendar. The
saying 'Don't cast a clout until May is out'
would result in very dirty clothes, a clout
being a piece of clothing. It has been
suggested that May refers to the month
rather than the flower.

The leaves are 5cm (2in) long and
mid-green, but they don't colour in
autumn. The deep pink, double flowers
appear in late spring, bending branches
with their weight. Unfortunately few
berries are produced and those that there
are, are small.

'Paul's Scarlet' is a great tree for
exposed, cold sites and is tolerant of air
pollution. Suckers may appear from below
the graft and should be removed as close
to the trunk as possible while small.

It will grow in all but waterlogged soil
with a maximum height and spread of
8m (26ft).

needs to be permanently staked. Unless
a leader is trained to form an upper
tier of weeping branches, the ultimate
height remains at 2m (6ft 6in) with a
similar spread.

Crataegus laciniata

CUT-LEAF HAWTHORN

If a hawthorn happens to grow in a field
in Ireland, away from the hedge or
boundary, it has the chance, short of a
lightning strike, to live for ever. No man
will lift his hand to harm, it for it is well
recognised by one and all as a fairy thorn,
where the 'little people', including fairies
and leprechauns, live. You may not believe
in a pot of gold at the end of a rainbow
but I dare you to uproot a fairy thorn.

Sometimes referred to as C. *orientalis*,
this Chinese hawthorn is less thorny than
native trees. When mature it forms a
compact, spreading, extremely hardy tree.

Crataegus x lavallei 'Carrierei'
HAWTHORN

This semi-evergreen tree has 10cm (4in) long, shiny, dark green, toothed leaves which, after a dry summer and autumn, turn red. In early summer the tree is covered with clusters of small, white flowers followed by orange-red berries, which last into winter. Displayed against the dark green leaves the berries light up a winter's day. This thorn can tolerate the poorest of soil, providing it is well drained. The plant will quickly grow to its maximum height of 7m (23ft) with a spread of 8m (26ft).

Cydonia oblonga
QUINCE

In Portugal the pulped fruit of quince is used to make marmelo, the origin of the marmalade we now make from citrus fruit. It is a deciduous tree with dark green 10cm

right
DAVIDIA INVOLUCRATA
A branch weighed down by the 'handkerchiefs' that give the plant one of its common names. The white 'flowers' are, in fact, bracts.

far right
EMBOTHRIUM COCCINEUM
The mass of scarlet flowers almost hides the foliage.

CYDONIA OBLONGA
The pale pink flowers make a charming show in spring, to be followed by pear-shaped fruit (see page 49).

(4in) long leaves, white felted on the underside turning to yellow in autumn. The pale pink or sometimes white flowers are 5cm (2in) across and appear at the leaf axils in late spring. The large, pear-shaped, pale green edible fruit turn to golden yellow in autumn. They are quite sour-tasting when raw, with a lemony fragrance. Best used for flavouring, the quince adds something to an apple pie that changes its flavour from ordinary to exceptional. They also make good preserves. Warm autumns are required to ripen the fruit and a well-drained soil is preferred. An old, mature tree may have a height and spread of 5m (16ft).

Davidia involucrata
GHOST TREE, HANDKERCHIEF TREE, DOVE TREE

If you have the space, this is a beautiful, conical, deciduous tree to grow. It dislikes being crowded or overhung by larger trees. The heart-shaped, hairy leaves are drawn out to a point, vivid green on the upper surface and densely felted underneath. In late spring, large white bracts appear, one on either side of the small, insignificant male flowers. The bracts are of unequal size. Seen fluttering in a breeze, it is easy to imagine how the tree came by its various common names. The flowers are followed by pendant, dirty-brown seed pods with a hard nut.

Davidia needs a moist, fertile soil in full sun to succeed. It is hardy but dislikes strong, cold winds. It will grow up to 15m (50ft) with a spread of 9m (30ft). *D. i. vilmoriniana* is similar but without hairs on the leaf surface and dark green on the underside. It is hardier than the species.

In 1899 Ernest Wilson was employed by Veitch's nursery in England to bring back a davidia. He travelled to China and, with a map drawn by Dr Agustine Henry, who lived 900 miles from the tree, Wilson searched for one davidia in an area larger than England. Eventually he found the stump – the tree had been cut down for timber. He wrote in his diary 'I did not sleep that night'. Fortunately, close by he found more trees and sent home seed.

Embothrium coccineum
CHILEAN FIRE BUSH

If only it were possible to grow this tree in every garden. It is one of the best evergreen gardening treasures, with its 12.5cm (5in) long, lance-shaped, dark green leaves as a backdrop to masses of tubular, scarlet flowers held in clusters during late spring and early summer. Unfortunately, it prefers a site sheltered from cold, drying winds and a moist, well drained, lime-free soil. Usually seen as a multi-stemmed plant it suckers freely, eventually forming a copse. It is not long-lived, but its offspring will be in flower before it deteriorates. It grows to a height of 10m (33ft) with a spread of 5m (16ft).

The form 'Lanceolatum Norquinco Valley' is hardier and will succeed in most areas of the British Isles. It is semi-evergreen with narrow leaves and the flowers cover the whole plant.

Eucalyptus gunnii

CIDER GUM

This Tasmanian eucalyptus is one of the hardiest of the species and has been in cultivation in England and North America for more than 100 years. Its young evergreen leaves are as well recognised as those of the chestnut or oak. The juvenile, first year, bright blue-green leaves are held in opposite pairs, rounded and without stalks. They almost appear to be one leaf, with the stem growing through the centre. Two year old, adult leaves are green-grey, up to 7.5cm (3in) long and lance-shaped.

EUCRYPHIA X NYMANSENSIS 'NYMANSAY' is grown for the fragrant flowers, rather like dog roses, that appear in late summer.

EUCALYPTUS PAUCIFLORA SUBSP. NIPHOPHILA displaying its patchwork bark.

The crushed foliage is strongly aromatic. The bark could be described as deciduous as, even with young trees, the outer layer peels and shreds, hanging in tatters to reveal a patchwork of white, cream, grey-green or even orange below. White flowers appear in clusters of three on short stalks at the leaf axil. They burst open in summer and autumn and are largely composed of white stamens.

The cider gum prefers a neutral to acid soil but will succeed on a chalk soil. All eucalypts are bad transplanters and are best planted in their permanent home when less than 60cm (2ft) high. Given a moist, free-draining soil they will grow 2m (6ft 6in) each year. If coppiced by cutting the stems 30cm (12in) from ground level, they will throw up strong 2m (6ft 6in) high stems of blue, juvenile foliage which is so beloved by florists. The timber is brittle and even large branches are prone to snap some distance from the trunk in a gale. Occasionally, in Britain, a severe frost will damage the foliage but the tree soon recovers. It grows to a height of 25m (80ft) with a spread of 15m (50ft).

Eucalyptus pauciflora subsp. niphophila

SNOW GUM, ALPINE SNOW GUM

If grown from seed collected from trees in the coldest parts of south-west Australia the resulting trees are well able to withstand the average British winter. In this species, the lance-shaped, leathery evergreen leaves have no juvenile form. The emerging aromatic foliage on young plants is orange-brown turning to sea-green. Young stems are covered in a waxy, silvery-white bloom, while the mature bark is blotched with green, grey and

surface mulch every spring. Slow growing with upright branches, it forms an open, round-headed tree up to 10m (33ft) high with a spread of 5m (16ft).

Eucryphia x intermedia 'Rostrevor'

It would not be fair to say that I included this tree because I love the County Down village of that name, nestling at the foot of the Mourne mountains and squeezed by Carlingford Lough but, like the village, it is memorable. The evergreen tree is spectacular in late summer. The glossy, dark green foliage is glaucous on the underside with both simple and pinnate leaves on the same plant. Shallow, cup-shaped, single, white flowers are pendulous and slightly smaller than those of *E. glutinosa*. In mid- to late summer they smother the tree, bending the slender stems. It likes a well-drained site sheltered from cold winds and eventually forms a columnar tree 10m (33ft) high with a spread of 6m (20ft).

cream. In summer there is a dazzling display of pure white flowers.

Snow gum will succeed best in an acid, free-draining soil. It is not a eucalypt that I would coppice, as its main attraction is its bark rather than the foliage. The snow gum is slow-growing for the first few years but once it has become established it will grow at least 1m (3ft) each year, eventually forming a round-headed tree with a height and spread of 6m (20ft).

EUCRYPHIA X INTERMEDIA 'ROSTREVOR' is free-flowering, with fragrant white flowers that plaster the tree in late summer.

Eucryphia glutinosa

It is a tree without a common name but 'beautiful' sounds about right. This species is deciduous or, in mild areas, semi-evergreen and is the hardiest of the eucryphia grown in Britain. In its native Chile it is evergreen. The pinnate leaves are made up of three to five glossy, dark green, toothed leaflets. In autumn they colour to orange-red and in a good year will remain for weeks before falling. The 5cm (2in) cup-shaped, fragrant, white flowers appear in mid- to late summer. Occasionally double flowers are produced. It prefers a sunny, sheltered site with its root area kept shaded and cool. Plant it in a free-draining neutral or acid soil and

Eucryphia x nymansensis 'Nymansay'

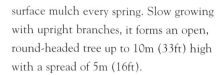

A stunning evergreen tree with glossy, dark green leaves that are pale green on the underside. Single and trifoliate leaflets appear on the same plant.

In late summer the tree is smothered with 7.5cm (3in), pure white, single, highly fragrant flowers not unlike those of a dog rose. The pronounced stamens are tipped with red anthers. It prefers a moist soil with its head in full sun and sheltered from cold winds. Unlike most eucryphia it is tolerant of an alkaline soil. This variety is fast-growing, forming a columnar tree with a height of 15m (50ft) and a spread of 5m (16ft).

Fagus

THE BEECH IS A MARVELLOUSLY ADAPTABLE tree. It is deciduous, forming a large, stately, round-headed shape. Unfortunately it is not a long-lived tree, usually blowing down or dying within 150 years. The timber is used for the manufacture of furniture. It is resistant to water damage so is ideal for boat building. It is suggested locally that Winchester cathedral in southern England was built on logs of beechwood on top of marshland. It may not be true but if it is, even beech will not last much longer than a thousand years.

FAGUS SYLVATICA

left
The usually silver-grey bark is occasionally fissured. I love to think that it is a defence against name carving.

above
One of the best trees for hedging, turning a glorious golden-brown colour in autumn and often retaining their leaves through the winter.

right
A truly impressive tree if you have the space to do it justice.

Fagus grandiflora
AMERICAN BEECH

A totally different tree from its European cousins (see right). It spreads by underground root suckers but for all that it is not a good traveller. It is unhappy growing in Europe, making a poor specimen of a tree.

The deciduous leaves are blue-green on the upper surface, paler on the underside. They have many more veins and are narrower and longer than those of the common beech. In autumn they turn a deep golden yellow. The smooth bark is noticeably paler in colour.

It is not fussy as to soil type, but dislikes waterlogged conditions. Slow-growing in Europe, it will form a bushy tree with a height and spread of 10m (33ft). In North America it has a better shape, usually pyramidal, growing to 30m (100ft) with a spread of 10m (33ft).

Fagus sylvatica

COMMON BEECH, EUROPEAN BEECH

A line of beeches at Meikleour, Perth in Scotland is claimed to be the tallest hedge in the world. It is over 30m (100ft) high and runs for more than 500m (600yd). The story behind the hedge is equally impressive. During the planting in 1745, the gardeners stopped their work to go and fight at the battle of Culloden. They never returned but to this day they have a monument erected by themselves.

The canopy of leaves on a mature beech is sufficiently dense to inhibit the growth of weeds or plants below. The young leaves are pale green and silky haired, becoming shiny, dark green and wavy edged. In autumn they turn to yellow and finally russet-brown before falling. Young hedges often retain some brown leaves over the winter months. The smooth, silvery-grey

bark is known to be the best for carving initials, a heart, or a lover's name. Not a practice to be encouraged, but the tree will live longer than the romance.

The male flowers are held in round clusters, the females in pairs. They develop into smooth or spiny shells which split in four, releasing two triangular seeds. These are known as mast and a year when there is a heavy crop of beech or oak seed is referred to as a 'mast year'. Providing the soil is well drained, a beech tree will grow on most soils including chalk. It dislikes transplanting and should be planted as a small tree. Beech is not suitable as a street tree because of its ultimate height of 25m (80ft) with a wide spread of over 15m (50ft).

Fagus sylvatica 'Aspleniifolia'

FERN-LEAVED BEECH, CUT-LEAF BEECH

In my book this tree is by far the most beautiful of the European beeches. It is slightly smaller than *F. sylvatica* and the deciduous foliage is more interesting. Each leaf is deeply cut, the lobes sharply pointed and fern-like. Grown in a well-drained soil or on a chalk site, the autumn colour is excellent with yellow, orange and russet shades preceding the traditional rich brown leaves. The stem structure differs from the common beech by having many more fine shoots on each branch. The tree's height at maturity is 20m (66ft) with a spread of 12m (40ft).

Look out for other varieties, including 'Incisa', which appears to have had its leaves shredded, 'Quercifolia' with oak-like leaves and slow-growing 'Rohanii', the purple fern-leaved beech.

above
FAGUS SYLVATICA
A beech wood in autumn is a memorable sight.

right
FAGUS SYLVATICA 'DAWYCK GOLD'
A narrow pillar of gold catching the evening sun.

Fagus sylvatica 'Dawyck Purple'

FASTIGIATE PURPLE BEECH

The original green-leaved *F. sylvatica* 'Dawyck' is a splendid, upright beech resembling in shape a Lombardy poplar (*Populus nigra* 'Italica') but considerably more attractive. It was found as a seedling at Dawyck estate in Scotland. The purple-leaved variety is the result of a chance cross between 'Dawyck' and a purple-leaved pollen parent. The wavy-edged deciduous leaves are a deep purple. Seen from a distance the tree appears to be black, while on closer inspection, on a bright day, it shimmers like purple silk. Its columnar shape makes it ideal for street planting where tree spread needs to be restricted. Two specimens on either side of an gateway set 2m (6ft 6in) back from the kerb will, in time, reward you with the most impressive entrance imaginable. It is best planted, as a young tree, in a deep, free-draining soil in full sun, in a position where its considerable height of 20m (66ft) will be appreciated. The spread at 4m (13ft) is more easily accommodated.

The variety 'Dawyck Gold' is similar, with golden rather than purple foliage.

Fagus sylvatica 'Purpurea Pendula'
WEEPING PURPLE BEECH

It would be difficult to dislike this small weeping beech. It is like an obedient child: you are sure it is going to misbehave but it doesn't. Usually top grafted, it may, on occasion, produce short green-leaved side shoots below the graft. These should be cut off as close to the main stem as possible to prevent others growing away from the stump. Plant it in a well-drained site in full sun and sheltered from cold winds.

The glossy purple-black leaves open late in spring but last well into autumn. It is slow-growing, forming a mushroom-shaped tree with a mature height and spread of 3m (10ft).

above
FAGUS SYLVATICA 'PURPUREA'
A matching pair of purple beech – a big tree, but magnificent if your garden can accommodate it.

right
FAGUS SYLVATICA 'PURPUREA PENDULA', in marked contrast to its upright relative, is small but perfectly formed.

Fraxinus excelsior 'Jaspidea'

GOLDEN ASH

A cultivar of the common ash (*F. excelsior*), the golden ash is just as slow to come into leaf. Country sages have tried to foretell the weather by the ash:

> 'Oak before the ash,
> you're in for a splash
> Ash before the oak,
> you're in for a soak.'

Whatever the weather, this tree gives of its best for all 12 months of the year. The 30cm (12in) long, pinnate leaves are a soft yellow in spring, becoming green. In autumn they again turn to a bright golden yellow before leaf fall. The yellow bark of the young stems highlights the jet black winter buds, while older bark is orange-yellow. Seen against a winter sky it gives a ghostly glow and in weak autumn sunlight the tree is ablaze with gold. In my garden's moist climate, the golden ash tends to suffer from canker. Pruning out the diseased branches encourages new growths, resulting in an unusual shaped tree with a crowded head of golden rods. In a moist, free-draining, slightly alkaline soil in full sun it will quickly form a large tree with a height of 20m (66ft) and a spread of 12m (40ft). In some nurseries and garden centres it is incorrectly named as 'Aurea', which is a slow-growing tree that is dwarf in habit. Make sure you purchase the correct plant.

The variety 'Pendula' is the weeping ash and the more gnarled it is the more I like it. I have to admit, though, it can be a sad and dejected looking tree. There is nothing uniform about it and it always seems to lurch to one side like Quasimodo. Come to think of it, the weeping ash is frequently found in church grounds and cemeteries.

FRAXINUS EXCELSIOR 'JASPIDEA'
gives value all year round, from the early
spring foliage (left) to the blazing autumn
colours (below).

The secret of selecting a good specimen
of weeping ash is to look for one that has
been grafted as high as possible on a
straight-stemmed common ash. If you have
to stand on a ladder to check, so much the
better. It will, in time, form a broad,
domed mound of pendulous branches, stiff
enough not to sway in the breeze. The
foliage is that of common ash with little
colouring in autumn before leaf fall.

Unfortunately this ash can not be
successfully grown in North America
where it suffers from many pests and
diseases. In Britain it enjoys a moist, free-
draining, alkaline soil growing to a height
of 15m (50ft) with a spread of 8m (26ft).

Genista aetnensis

MOUNT ETNA BROOM

There are those who argue that this and
all other brooms are shrubs. In defence, I
would point out that it will, with the help
of a sheltering wall, easily reach 7-8m (23-
26ft). Old, gnarled plants growing halfway
up the slopes of Mount Etna are an
astonishing sight and are certainly trees. It
is a deciduous tree with weeping branches
and bright green shoots which, as they
age, become devoid of leaves. Young stems
carry thin, rush-like foliage which soon
falls off. In mid- to late summer fragrant,
pea-shaped, golden yellow flowers appear
at the tips of the shoots.

Many plants are short-lived, suffering
from a fungal disease that causes dieback.
When the season is hot and dry, rust
disease can strike. Prune as little as
possible, as hard cutting may cause a tree
to die. This broom grows best in a free-
draining, impoverished soil in a sheltered
site in full sun. It tolerates a soil over-
lying chalk.

Gleditsia triacanthos

HONEY LOCUST

Widely planted in North America and in Mediterranean areas, the green-leaved original species G. *triacanthos* has been largely neglected in Britain. 'Triacanthos' refers to the bunches of vicious 10-15cm (4-6 in) long, needle-sharp thorns that adorn its trunk and branches. The variety 'Sunburst' is thornless, which explains its popularity. It forms a beautiful, open, deciduous tree and being thornless is ideal as a street tree or as a specimen plant in a shrub bed. The open branch structure allows daylight to penetrate to any underplanting. Pinnate leaves appear in spring, a startling, bright, shining gold, turning to pale green-yellow in summer. In autumn they change again to a soft yellow. Unlike its parent, 'Sunburst' doesn't produce long seed pods. In a free-draining, fertile soil this tree will perform well but it requires a sheltered site in full sun. Late spring frosts may damage new growths. Where branch removal is necessary, the tree should not be pruned before autumn or it will bleed. It is a fast-growing tree forming a conical head with a height and spread of 10m (33ft).

The variety 'Elegantissima' makes a smaller, more compact tree. It is slower-growing with bright green leaves and no thorns. It will grow to a height of 7m (23ft) with a spread of 5m (16ft).

Halesia monticola

SNOWDROP TREE, MOUNTAIN SILVERBELL

An American native, the silverbell didn't arrive in Britain until the reign of Queen Victoria. We promptly gave it the name of snowdrop tree and, in truth, the flowers

above
GLEDITSIA TRIACANTHOS
– a tree that deserves to be better known. It needs a sheltered site and lots of sunshine.

right
HALESIA MONTICOLA
The 'snowdrop' flowers appear at the same time as the opening leaves.

are as much like a snowdrop as a silverbell. It has settled well and is a hardy, fast-growing tree in all areas of Britain. It is deciduous with 20cm (8in) long, light green leaves that are downy when young but hairless as they age and turning pale yellow in autumn. The clusters of pure white, 2.5cm (1in) long, bell-shaped flowers appear in spring, before or at the same time as the leaves. They make a spectacular display for two to three weeks and are followed by 5cm (2in) long, green, bell-shaped, four-winged fruit. These are reluctant to drop and are often still

hanging at the same time as the following year's flowers. The form *H. monticola* f. *rosea* has pale pink flowers, while *H. m* var. *vestita* produces larger white, or occasionally pink, flowers.

The snowdrop tree prefers an open, free-draining slightly acid soil sheltered from cold winds. It is immune to most pests and diseases. Its ultimate height in Britain is 12m (40ft) with a spread of 8m (26ft). In the Smoky Mountains of the south-eastern United States, where it enjoys moist, well-drained, lime-free soil, *Halesia monticola* may reach 30m (100ft).

Hamamelis mollis

CHINESE WITCH HAZEL

This deciduous shrub or small tree is not a hazel at all, although its leaves are shaped like those of a nut-bearing hazel, pale green in summer, turning butter-yellow in autumn. The frost-resistant winter flowers are delightfully fragrant. They are a curious shape, resembling a spider with legs made from thin, golden-yellow strips of lemon peel.

Hamamelis mollis prefers a moist, well-drained, acid soil in a sunny site, but tolerates light shade and a neutral soil. When mature it forms a broad head with the lower branches almost horizontal. It grows to a height and spread of 4m (13ft).

Hippophae rhamnoides

SEA BUCKTHORN

This is one tree whose common name aptly describes the plant. An excellent choice for coastal sites, it will even survive in sand at any point above the high-tide mark. When grown as a hedge the thorns are a good deterrent. It will grow in almost anything except waterlogged ground but prefers an alkaline soil in full sun. Trees are deciduous with silver, 5cm (2in) long leaves. Female plants need to be close to a male for pollination. Insignificant, greenish yellow flowers open in spring and are followed in autumn by masses of round, orange-yellow berries. They are beautifully highlighted by the silver foliage and after a shower of rain the whole plant appears to glow. The juicy fruit is sufficiently acid to deter birds from eating it, allowing the tree to provide show and pleasure for most of the winter. Older branches have a habit of splitting but, if undamaged, the tree will grow to a height and spread of 6m (20ft).

Hoheria angustifolia

This beautiful evergreen tree is native to New Zealand. Unfortunately it is slightly tender and needs a sheltered garden to perform well. It is columnar in habit with 2.5cm (1in) long glossy, deep-green leaves with a toothed edge. The fragrant, cup-shaped white flowers appear in the leaf axils in late summer and are a great attraction for butterflies.

left

HAMAMELIS MOLLIS
There are those who claim the witch hazel is a shrub. I am happy to think of this as a tree.

above

HOHERIA ANGUSTIFOLIA
A fragrant white-flowering tree is a bonus in any garden in late autumn.

The ideal time to plant hoheria is in late spring. When pruning is necessary to maintain the tree's shape, it should be carried out at this time too. Surface mulching every spring will keep the root area cool.

The soil needs to be well drained, alkaline and in full sun. In a site well sheltered from cold winds and frost, this slow-growing tree will reach a height of 7m (23ft) spreading by as much as 3m (10ft).

Ilex

NATIVE TO MOST OF EUROPE, THE HOLLY has been revered since long before Christianity; it was used in ancient pagan rites and is no less highly regarded today. Christmas wouldn't be the same without sprigs of its bright red berries for decoration, while the conical evergreen tree laden with berries is a wonderful sight against a backdrop of a crisp, pale blue winter sky.

The spiny evergreen foliage of the English holly (*Ilex aquifolium*) makes it ideal for hedging, either on its own or mixed with deciduous hawthorn or beech. As an ornamental, holly has lots of competition from other trees, but few equals. There are variegated hollies, blue-green hollies and hollies with spineless foliage. The fruit, which is mildly poisonous, colours up in late summer to orange-red, deep red or yellow, depending on the variety. Although *I. aquifolium* is not hardy enough for some areas of North America, the American species *I. opaca*, with its matt green leaves, can withstand the British climate.

Hollies are not fussy as to site or soil conditions, although they prefer an open site, sheltered from biting cold winds. Most soils are adequate providing they don't become waterlogged for long periods. When planting, fork up the base of the hole to allow water to drain. Incorporate lots of old compost or rotted farmyard manure.

One piece of advice I must pass on. Underplant your holly with a good ground-covering plant that doesn't require weeding. It takes holly leaves forever to rot down and their spines are a serious nuisance to bare hands.

ILEX AQUIFOLIUM 'BACCIFLAVA' bears yellow berries which are less likely to be eaten by birds.

Ilex x altaclerensis 'Golden King'
VARIEGATED HOLLY

Most hollies carry male and female flowers on different plants. To obtain a crop of berries, the female flowers need to be pollinated. Isn't it daft then that a female variety should be named 'Golden King'? I suppose, to be politically correct, a male variety has been named 'Golden Queen'. 'Golden King' is one of the Highclere hybrids, all crosses between the English holly, *Ilex aquifolium* and *I. perado*, from Madeira. The resulting trees are more vigorous and their leaves less spiny than English holly.

The 10cm (4in) long, evergreen leaves of 'Golden King' are frequently spineless. They are grey-green with a broad, bright gold margin. Occasionally growths with only yellow leaves will appear. Small, white, single-sex flowers appear in early summer followed by dull brown-red berries which quickly turn bright red. They are usually sparsely distributed over the tree. It will grow in most soils including alkaline, providing it is moist and free-draining. If grown in a sunny position the variegation will be improved. High levels of air pollution are tolerated and it enjoys coastal gardens. 'Golden King' is ideal for a hedge and if mixed with a few male plants it will produce berries. Trees are fast-growing, reaching 6m (20ft) with a spread of 4m (13ft).

Ilex aquifolium
ENGLISH HOLLY, COMMON HOLLY, HOLY TREE

One of the most common of Britain's native evergreens, holly has been used through the ages as a cure-all, for timber carving and as a decoration to celebrate

Christmas. The berries are slightly poisonous, yet birds love them and strip my trees long before December. The glossy, dark green leaves are variable and may be wavy or smooth, with or without spines. Tight clusters of white flowers appear in early summer, males and females on separate plants. When pollination occurs the female produces bright red berries. With some varieties the berries may be yellow, for example 'Amber' and 'Bacciflava'.

This evergreen tree is as tough as old boots. In exposed areas it makes a wonderful high sheltering screen or hedge. Imagine a mixed hedge planted with common holly and deciduous beech – the combination of weak winter sunlight on the brown, dead beech leaves and the glossy, dark green holly, plus the bonus of glistening, bright red berries. That is what I would call a good design detail.

Avoid planting on soil that becomes waterlogged. Holly trees dislike being transplanted so purchase a small bare-rooted or container-grown plant. It will form an erect tree with a height of 25m (80ft) and a spread of 7m (23ft).

Ilex aquifolium 'Ferox Argentea'
VARIEGATED HEDGEHOG HOLLY, SILVER HEDGEHOG HOLLY

This variety of the English holly is male but don't allow that to put you off. Its absence of berries is more than compensated for by its extraordinary, evergreen leaves.

The upper surface of the small, hunch-backed leaves have creamy-white margins and are covered with vicious sharp spines. Hence 'ferox', the fierce. A good piece of advice is to avoid having to weed by hand under this English holly tree. Slower growing than *I. aquifolium*, this variety

ILEX AQUIFOLIUM 'ARGENTEA MARGINATA PENDULA'
A slow-growing weeping female variety, with each leaf perfectly margined in creamy white.

makes a marvellous garden hedge. The young stems are purple, contrasting with the variegation of the foliage. Hedge clipping should be carried out in spring. It will grow in most sites, with the exception of waterlogged ground, and is recommended for acid soils. Its ultimate height is 8m (26ft) with a spread of 4m (13ft).

Ilex aquifolium 'J. C. van Tol'

This is one sexy holly. Unlike most other varieties, 'J. C. van Tol' carries male and female flowers on the same plant. As a result of self-pollination, it is usually laden with bright, Santa-Claus red berries. The 7.5cm (3in) long, glossy, dark, evergreen leaves are slightly puckered but are spineless or, at any rate, almost spineless. The young shoots are dark purple. Birds love the berries and if a supply is required for winter decoration you will have to reserve them early by covering ripe clusters with a muslin bag. With an annual display of berries almost guaranteed, plant the tree in a prominent position. It will thrive in almost any soil but if the site is free-draining, moist and fertile it will repay you with fast growth, making a broad-based upright tree 7m (23ft) high and spreading to 4m (13ft).

Juglans regia

COMMON WALNUT, JOVE'S NUTS

Juglans is derived from *Jovis glans* or 'Jupiter's acorn'. The Romans loved this tree and it is generally agreed that it was brought to Britain by their army. To them Jupiter was an important god so they probably offered him their favourite titbit. The timber, much in demand for furniture, has great value. The branches are usually twisted with smooth, silver bark, later becoming deeply fissured. The deciduous, pinnate leaves unfurl orange in late spring. They become pale brown before turning a deep, glossy green and finally a disappointing brown in autumn. When crushed they are strongly aromatic, acting as a deterrent to flies. *J. regia* is the only walnut with leaves without a serrated edge.

The green-yellow catkins, male and female, are carried separately on the same tree, appearing with the leaves in late spring. The nuts are encased in a spherical, thick, furrowed shell. Varieties have been selected for their flavour and crop size. A favourite is the French variety 'Franquette'. 'Buccaneer' and 'Broadview' are two early fruiting varieties.

The tree succeeds best in a deep, fertile, well-drained soil in full sun. Avoid areas prone to late frosts. It dislikes transplanting, so purchase a small plant in a container and plant it in its permanent position. Where pruning is necessary to shape the tree it should be undertaken in late summer to prevent bleeding. Overall height may be 30m (100ft) with a spread exceeding 20m (66ft).

above
JUGLANS REGIA
The male catkins are striking as the leaves emerge.

right
KOELREUTERIA PANICULATA
bears large panicles of golden flowers, followed in autumn by bladder-like fruit.

Koelreuteria paniculata

GOLDEN RAIN TREE, PRIDE OF INDIA

It may well be the pride of India but this is a Chinese tree. The deciduous leaves are pinnate, each lobed leaflet resembling an oak leaf. The young leaves are pale red at first, becoming light green. In autumn they turn a soft yellow for a brief few days. It flowers in late summer when few other trees are in bloom, producing large, 30cm (12in) panicles of small, yellow flowers. They are followed by 5cm (2in) bladder-shaped seed pods, green at first, turning pink and then brown. It prefers a well-drained soil and will succeed in alkaline conditions. Plant it in a sunny site sheltered from cold winds. It forms a spreading tree 10m (33ft) high with a spread of 9m (30ft).

x Laburnocytisus adamii
ADAM'S LABURNUM

If you are the type of gardener who likes to be able to show something different to your friends (and who doesn't?), then this is the tree for you. It is the result of a graft made by a Parisian nurseryman, a Monsieur Adam in 1825. He successfully grafted the dwarf, purple broom, *Cytisus purpureus*, on to the common laburnum, *Laburnum anagyroides*. The result is what is known as a chimera, a graft hybrid, rather than a hybrid brought about by cross pollination.

A deciduous tree with dark green, three-palmate leaves, it has pea-like flowers in late spring that are a mixture of the two parents. There are the typical yellow laburnum flowers along with dense, purple clusters of the broom. There are also coppery-pink flowers, a mixture of the two. Personally I think it is a disaster. The tree, for most of the year, looks diseased and about to die (of shame). For the few weeks when it is in full colour I find it sore on the eyes.

Its ideal site is in full sun in a moist, well-drained soil. It is prone to sucker and these should be removed as soon as they are noticed. It will grow to 8m (26ft) with a spread of 5m (16ft).

Laburnum alpinum
SCOTCH LABURNUM

How or why it got the name of Scotch I have no idea. It's not a whisky, broth or mist. It is, however, hardy enough to succeed in Scotland. Its deciduous, glossy, dark green, palmate leaves are pale green on the underside and turn to yellow in autumn. Long racemes of drooping, bright, yellow, pea-like flowers are fragrant during early summer. They are followed by flattened pods of poisonous seeds.

It prefers a sunny situation and thrives in alkaline soil that is free-draining. It tolerates pollution, making it ideal for inner-city gardens. The tree has an upright habit with stiff branches and an eventual height and spread of 7m (23ft).

Laburnum x watereri 'Vossii'
GOLDEN RAIN

A truly beautiful tree when in flower. The dark green three-palmate leaves are hairy on the underside. They provide a backdrop for the 50cm (20in) long trailing racemes of golden flowers in late spring and early summer. The scarce seed pods are usually sterile and are brown, turning black. This is the best of all the laburnums and makes a magnificent display when trained over an arch or pergola and viewed from below. It needs a well-drained soil in full sun and has an ultimate height and spread of 9m (29ft).

Liquidambar styraciflua
SWEET GUM

In Britain they are simply called liquidambars. In North America they are known as sweet gums. In either case the trees deserve better: perhaps 'flaming torch' or 'glowing autumn', for they can be truly spectacular before leaf fall. The bark, even on young plants, is raised and corky. The deciduous, glossy green, five- to seven-lobed foliage could easily be confused with that of a maple but the leaves are arranged alternately along the stem, whereas maple leaves are opposite.

Small green-yellow flowers appear in spring, the males in groups of three on the same tree as the clusters of females. Small, spiky fruit follow in autumn. For autumn

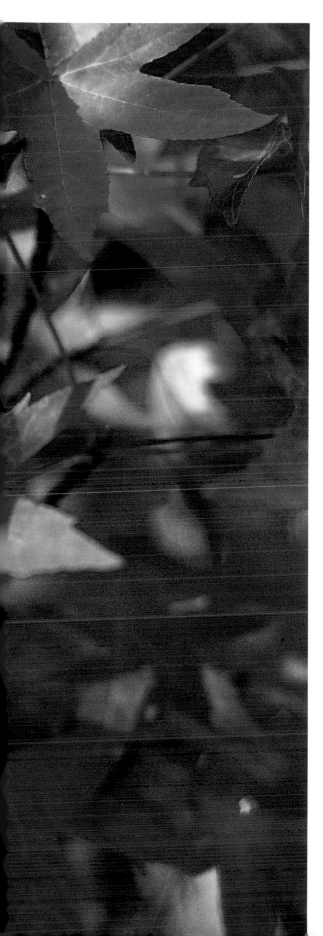

left

LIQUIDAMBAR STYRACIFLUA
Maple-like foliage colours in autumn like an enormous flaming torch, carpeting the ground after leaf fall.

below

LIRIODENDRON TULIPIFERA
Unusual in leaf and flower, this tree would try the patience of a saint – you will probably have to wait upwards of 20 years before you see a single bloom.

colour this tree gives of its best. Even in an off year the colour is good and individual leaves may be orange, bright red or deepest maroon. Selections that emphasize prominent colours are offered by some nurseries: 'Lane Roberts', a rich dark crimson; 'Palo Alto', a bright orange; and 'Worplesdon', with deeply lobed leaves that turn purple and finally orange-yellow.

Liquidambar prefers a deep, wet but not waterlogged soil, slightly acid, in full sun. If the soil is deep it will tolerate an alkaline soil. The fleshy roots dislike transplanting once established. Basal suckers may be a problem. If pruning is necessary, complete the operation by autumn to prevent bleeding. Slow growing, it will, in time, form a large, bushy tree 20m (66ft) high with a spread of 10m (33ft).

Liriodendron tulipifera 'Aureomarginatum'

VARIEGATED TULIP TREE

A magnificent deciduous tree but I do wish it would flower earlier in the season and in its life. Once you have seen the leaves you will always recognise them. They appear to have had the tip bitten off. They are almost square with lobes at the 'bitten' end and one shallow lobe to each side. In this variety they are deep green with a broad margin of bright yellow. In autumn they turn pale yellow, then fall, carpeting the ground in green-gold.

The unusual and interesting flowers appear in early summer. They are cup-shaped, 5cm (2in) long, resembling a pale-green tulip with a band of orange at the base. Cone-like, pale brown fruit appear in autumn, often remaining on the tree until spring. The tree is usually 20-25

years old before it flowers and frustratingly it does so in summer when it is in full leaf and the flowers are not easily seen from the ground.

Late spring planting is preferable, as a container-grown plant, as young specimens are susceptible to frost. The roots are fleshy and easily damaged. It prefers a soil that doesn't dry out or become hot. At the other extreme it won't survive in waterlogged conditions. A fertile, slightly acid soil is best. The tulip tree will grow to 18m (60ft) with a spread of 10m (33ft).

Lomatia ferruginea

This forms a beautiful, small evergreen tree with red-brown, felted stems. The dark green, pinnate leaves are made up of lobed, lance-shaped, leaflets. They are pale brown and are also felted on the underside. The flowers appear in mid-summer, as 5cm (2in) pendulous racemes. Each flower is yellow-brown and deep red. The tree grows best in a deep, well-drained, acid soil in sun or light shade. It is not totally hardy, needing protection from cold winds and hard frosts. Its ultimate height is 9m (30ft) spreading to 5m (16ft).

Luma apiculata

MYRTLE

This great evergreen used to be called *Myrtus luma* but fortunately only the name has changed. In the south-west of Ireland, with its mild and humid climate, this tree has become naturalized. At my home in County Down, Northern Ireland, it self-seeds profusely. There are only so many that can be given to church sales; the remainder are treated as posh weeds.

The first thing you notice is the cinnamon-coloured bark which, even on young trees, peels in long patches to expose the creamy-white inner surface. The 2.5cm (1in) long, dull, dark green, highly aromatic leaves are pale green on the underside. Pink and green flower buds appear at the leaf axils. From mid-summer through until mid-autumn the tree is covered with small white flowers that contrast with the dark foliage. The small purple-black fruit ripen in late autumn and are edible and quite sweet.

Grow it in a well-drained soil with added humus in the form of old manure or compost. It will tolerate an alkaline soil. Site in full sun and sheltered from cold winds and frost. In a suitable climate the myrtle makes a wonderful evergreen hedge. Free-standing, it will grow to a height of 6m (20ft) spreading to 4m (13ft).

Maackia amurensis

A charming, slow growing tree deserving of better recognition. The deciduous, pinnate, dark- green leaves are 20 -30cm (8 -12in) long and paler on the underside. The new spring growths are pale grey. The tree comes into flower from an early age during mid to late summer. The erect racemes of pea-like flowers are white with a hint of pale grey-blue. They are followed by 5cm (2in) long straight pods holding up to five seeds. To flower well it needs to be planted in a deep, fertile, neutral to acid soil in full sun. Where there is a good depth of topsoil, it may be grown over chalk. It will grow to 15m (50ft) high with a spread of 9m (30ft).

left
LIRIODENDRON TULIPIFERA
'AUREOMARGINATUM'
makes a good specimen tree for the lawn while you wait for it to flower.

below
MAACKIA AMURENSIS
Even young trees flower and produce see-through pods of seed.

Magnolia delavayi

A truly magnificent flowering evergreen magnolia from China. Its 30cm (12in) long leaves unfurl a coppery-brown quickly becoming dull mid-green on the upper surface and pale green on the underside. The rough, corky bark is creamy-white and stands out against the foliage. Large, 20cm (8in), creamy-white flowers appear in late summer. They resemble cups made of parchment and are slightly fragrant. Unfortunately the flowers are not prolific and are short lived, lasting only two days.

In all but the most favourable climates this tree will need a sheltered situation. It will grow beautifully and make a fine display on a red brick wall facing the evening sun. It prefers a moist, deep, humus-rich soil in sun or partial shade but, unlike most magnolias, will tolerate dry conditions and an alkaline soil.

Magnolias have a habit of forming branches close to ground level resulting in a bushy shape. The lower side branches may be pruned in summer to encourage the main leader to form a tree up to 10m (33ft) high with a wide spread of 9m (30ft).

Magnolia grandiflora 'Little Gem'
BULL BAY

Whoever thought up the common name of bull bay was seriously lacking in imagination. If you would love to grow the species *Magnolia grandiflora* but haven't the space, then this is the tree for you. It is evergreen, with 15cm (6in) long leaves, glossy, dark green on the upper surface, felted, dark brown on the underside. The leaves are easily dried and last for years, looking as though picked fresh the previous day. The 10cm (4in) creamy-white, delightfully fragrant flowers appear in summer and early autumn.

'Little Gem' thrives in a moist, well-drained neutral to acid soil with lots of added leaf mould but will tolerate an alkaline soil, providing it has a deep root run. It needs a sheltered site with protection from cold winds, growing well on a wall that catches the evening sun, where it will slowly reach 6m (19ft) with a spread of 3m (10ft).

Magnolia kobus

This tree is well worth waiting for. I have to mention that at the start, since patience is needed for the 12-15 year wait it takes to produce its first flower. Don't you dare score it off the list. It is a deciduous magnolia with 20cm (8in) long, aromatic, mid-green leaves and downy flower buds. The spring flowers are goblet- or saucer-shaped, up to 10cm (4in) across and pure white, occasionally flushed with pink towards the base. Once this Japanese tree does finally decide to flower, it does so with carefree abandon, producing masses of bloom.

It is a hardy tree, succeeding in all but the most exposed sites in Britain. Plant it

in sun or shade in a deep, free-draining alkaline or acid soil. It grows 30cm (12in) a year to form a broad-headed tree 12m (40ft) high with a spread of 9m (30ft).

Magnolia 'Wada's Memory'

SWEET BAY

 This tree is named for the breeder, Mr K. Wada of Japan who supplied it to the University of Washington Arboretum, Seattle. It forms a deciduous tree. The advantage, I feel, is all ours, with the flowers making their appearance before the foliage. The 15cm (6in) leaves are bronze when young, quickly turning to deep, glossy green. During mid- to late spring the 15cm (6in) pure white, fragrant, cup-shaped flowers appear in profusion. It is fully hardy although the flowers may be damaged by a late frost.

The roots of all magnolias are quite brittle, so care should be taken when planting them. A moist or wet, but not waterlogged, fertile soil enriched with leaf mould and compost is ideal. Mulch annually with compost or rotted farmyard manure. Magnolias cannot tolerate an alkaline soil. In Britain the eventual height of 'Wada's Memory' is 9m (30ft) with a spread of 7m (23ft).

left

MAGNOLIA KOBUS

Emerging flowers resemble a haze of white butterflies.

above

MAGNOLIA KOBUS

In autumn, the ripe seed pods burst open to show off the bright red seeds.

Malus

THE CRAB APPLE IS ONE OF OUR MOST useful and colourful garden trees. They are all deciduous, with varieties to suit the smallest garden. In spring they produce single or double, often fragrant, flowers in white, pink or red, followed in autumn by bountiful crops of fruit. Fruit size varies but 5cm (2in) is common; they may be yellow (*Malus* 'Golden Hornet') through to red-purple (*Malus pumila* 'Cowichan'). Often this colourful display is brought to an abrupt end when the crab apples become food for our garden birds. If you manage to harvest some fruit, crab apple jelly has a taste of its own. Some varieties of malus, such as 'Profusion', have young purple foliage, and these colour best in full sun.

Crab apple trees are hardy in all parts of the British Isles. Biting cold winds and late spring frosts may damage early blossom and reduce the insect population needed for pollination, resulting in a lack of fruit.

Crab apples are not fussy and will grow on any soil with the exception of waterlogged sites. They prefer a well-drained, fertile soil in sun or partial shade.

below
MALUS FLORIBUNDA
Red buds quickly open to pale pink blossom in such a mass as to hide the leaves.

right
MALUS 'COWICHAN'
The rose-pink flower buds gradually open to white. The red-purple young leaves turn dark green in summer.

Malus floribunda

JAPANESE CRAB APPLE

There are better crab apples but none as memorable in flower. The small 7.5cm (3in) dull, dark-green, deciduous leaves almost disappear during flowering in mid-spring, when the cherry-red flower buds open to reveal the white insides of the petals. This combination of closed and open flowers produces a startling display of red, pink and white. Until you have witnessed the show it is impossible to imagine such a mass of colour on a single tree. The spectacle is repeated annually, each year being better than its predecessor without any 'off' seasons. The red or yellow pea-sized fruit that follow the flowers are plentiful but disappointingly small. Hungry birds soon remove them.

M. *floribunda* is one of the earliest-flowering crab apples. Unless the site is sheltered from cold winds the blossom may suffer from air frost, resulting in a poor crop. It prefers a site in full sun in a moist, free-draining, fertile soil. At maturity it forms a spreading tree with arching branches. The height and spread may be 10m (33ft).

Malus 'Golden Hornet'
GOLDEN CRAB APPLE

A must for every small garden, if only to see how wide a blackbird's beak can open to hold one of the bright yellow apples. The deciduous, 10cm (4in) long, toothed leaves are bright green. In late spring pale pink buds open to white flowers and are followed by masses of 2.5cm (1in) bright yellow crab apples. The fruit are long lasting: if the birds leave them alone and they don't rot as a result of scab disease, the branches will remain laden until after Christmas. The fruit makes a wonderful clear jelly.

'Golden Hornet' is hardy and prefers a site in full sun. It will grow on most soils except those which are waterlogged. A spring feed of fertilizer which is high in potash will encourage a good crop of fruiting branches. It forms a round-headed tree 10m (33ft) high with a spread of 7m (23ft).

Malus 'John Downie'

This is the best of the crab apples for fruit. You can eat it from the tree without it bringing a tear to your eye. The large, 10cm (4in), glossy green leaves make a suitable backdrop for the small pink flower buds, which open to pure white in late spring. The show of blossom isn't spectacular but the display of fruit in the autumn more than compensates. The 2.5cm (1in) ovoid fruit hang in bunches on long stalks.

Their glossy skin ripens from yellow through orange to red and scarlet. In villages up and down the length of England, pots of jelly made from this crab apple vie for first prize at the local show.

'John Downie' will grow in most sites but there is less risk of canker disease in a well drained soil. Don't plant it in low-lying ground where the blossom will be at risk from late spring frosts. Young trees have ascending branches which, in maturity, broaden out to form a broad-headed tree 9m (30ft) high with a spread of 5m (16ft).

Malus 'Neville Copeman'

This variety of crab deserves a place in the larger garden. Tree shape, leaf, flower and fruit help make it a good all-rounder. The 10cm (4in) long leaves are purple-red when they first open, turning to dark

left
MALUS 'PROFUSION'
Dark purple-red flowers smother the tree, followed by deep red persistent fruit.

above
MALUS X ROBUSTA 'RED SENTINEL'
White flowers are followed by deep glossy red fruit ideal for making jelly.

far right
MALUS 'NEVILLE COPEMAN'
The young purple-red leaves make an ideal backdrop for the deep pink flowers.

green with a hint of purple in summer. Dark, wine red-pink flowers appear in clusters in late spring, followed by conical orange-red fruit, some of which ripen to a deep crimson. The fruit is very sour, but makes a well-flavoured jelly.

Fruit colour is improved when grown in a well-drained soil in full sun. Shelter from cold winds is necessary to protect the blossom. It matures to a large, spreading tree with a height and spread of 9m (30ft).

Malus 'Profusion'

If deep red is your favourite colour, then plant this tree. The deciduous 7.5cm (3in) long leaves open a deep purple-red, turning to coppery-green as they age. The young shoots are deep red. The 5cm (2in), fragrant, dark purple-pink flowers appear in late spring in large clusters, completely covering the tree. The blossom is followed by small, cherry-sized, deep red fruit which persist well into winter. They are not enjoyable to eat and I have never seen them used for jelly.

The tree will grow well in most soils with the exception of waterlogged ground, and prefers a site in full sun. The growing habit is upright when the tree is young, later spreading to form a tree with a height and spread of 9m (30ft).

Malus pumila 'Dartmouth'

As a young tree it is vigorous and upright, later maturing to a rounded shape with an open head. The large, deciduous, dark green leaves are up to 10cm (4in) long. In late spring pink buds open to white flowers, followed in autumn by large 5cm (2in) round, deep purple fruit which lasts well into winter. It will grow to a height of 8m (26ft) with a spread of 7m (23ft).

Malus x robusta 'Red Sentinel'

A very hardy tree with 7.5cm (3in) long, deep green leaves. There are masses of white flowers in late spring followed by small yellow-red fruit which later change colour to a glossy, deep red. The tree will hold its fruit well into winter. It prefers a deep, moist soil in a sunny situation. Watch out for canker disease which will kill off the smallest of branches and fruiting spurs. A spreading tree, it will, at maturity, grow to 7m (23ft) with a spread of 6m (20ft).

Malus 'Royal Beauty'

This is the best weeping crab apple forming a small compact tree with trailing, purple-red stems. The deciduous, 5cm (2in) red-purple leaves turn to dark green in early summer with purple undersides. The deep red-purple flowers appear in late spring and are followed in autumn by small, dark red fruit that persist into winter. It prefers a moist, deep, fertile soil in a sunny position. Regular pruning will produce a dense canopy of fruiting stems with a height and spread of 2m (6ft 6in).

Mespilus germanica

MEDLAR

If grown as a specimen it is worth raising the tree's twisted head by removing the lower branches. This allows enough light through the canopy for grass to grow and be cut. The long, softly hairy, mid-green, deciduous leaves colour to russet in autumn. Large 5cm (2in) white or pink-white, bowl-shaped flowers appear at the tips of shoots in late spring.

Medlar fruits form behind the flower in the same way as rosehips do, but the end away from the stalk remains open, giving them a distinctive appearance. Apple-shaped, they are 5cm (2in) across and brown when ripe. They are only edible when they have been 'bletted' by a few frosts. Put crudely, you eat them when they are half rotten. I would eat them for a dare – and if you want an after-dinner discussion serve them for dessert. There are two varieties available, both with smaller fruit, 'Nottingham' and 'Dutch', which has russet-brown fruit.

The medlar is totally hardy, tolerating most soils with the exception of very wet. Immune to cold winds, it will succeed in sun or light shade. Growing to just 5m (16ft) in height, this tree is a spreader covering 8m (26ft) when mature.

Morus nigra

BLACK MULBERRY

When I think of mulberries, I visualize silkworm caterpillars eating the leaves to produce silk. The trouble is, it's the white mulberry, *Morus alba*, that they eat. The black mulberry is best known for its raspberry-like fruit, with a taste that is acid and sweet at the same time. It has unjustly become a neglected plant in recent years.

above
MORUS NIGRA
The bitter-sweet fruit of the black mulberry.

right
NOTHOFAGUS ANTARCTICA
Small crinkled leaves shine in sunlight and rain.

The deciduous, 15cm (6in) long leaves are heart-shaped and mid-green with a rough, textured upper surface. In autumn they become pale, finally turning bright, buttercup yellow. In spring, small, green, cup-shaped male and female flowers appear in separate catkins on the same plant. The female clusters turn into 2.5cm (1in) long, green fruit. In autumn the fruits colour to red and then deep purple. At any one time there will be pale green, red, purple and almost black fruit on the same tree, which looks attractive but makes harvesting difficult. I find it hard to describe their flavour. Even when fully ripe, mulberries have a sharp taste, but they are sweet rather than acid. Eat one and see if you think of anything better. Unfortunately there is a 20-year wait before a tree commences cropping.

The scaly bark is dull orange with a gnarled, twisted look long before its time.

Propagation could not be more simple. Cut a large branch up to 2m (6ft 6in) long in the autumn and push it to a depth of at least 45cm (18in) into a hole in the ground made with a crowbar. Some coarse grit in the base of the hole will prevent waterlogging. Firm the 'cutting' in and check regularly that it isn't loosened by wind. That way you may have fruit inside 15 years. Take my advice and don't plant your mulberry as a specimen in the lawn or on the patio. Birds eating the fruit in the tree will cause an awful mess on the grass and permanently stain the patio surface.

The mulberry will thrive on most soils with the exception of waterlogged ground. It needs a site in full sun and a good warm autumn to ripen the fruit. It slowly forms a round-headed tree 12m (40ft) high with a spread of 13m (43ft).

Nothofagus antarctica
ANTARCTICA BEECH

Southern beeches are in a class of their own. They are as deserving of a place in our gardens as the northern hemisphere beech, *Fagus sylvatica* (see page 149). The 2.5cm (1in) long, deciduous, glossy, dark green leaves are crinkled with toothed edges. They are carried on either side of the thin stems. In autumn they turn

bright yellow and then brown. The flowers are insignificant, hanging in small, yellow clusters in spring.

They prefer deep, moist, well-drained ground. Unlike *Fagus sylvatica*, Nothofagus cannot tolerate an alkaline soil. It is hardy and resistant to cold winds and exposure. If not trained, it tends to form a multi-stemmed, bushy tree with a lot of midriff bulge. It will grow to 15m (50ft) high with a spread of 8m (26ft).

NYSSA SYLVATICA
The autumn colour is spectacular after a long, hot summer – once every ten years or so in my garden!

Nyssa sylvatica
TUPELO, BLACK GUM

The ancient Greeks knew a thing or two; they had Nyssa down as a nymph who enjoyed water. And this tree loves a wet or swampland site. Planted close to a lake it – and its reflection – is breathtaking in autumn. The oval, pointed 15cm (6in) leaves are usually a dark glossy green but occasionally the upper surface is a dull paler green. In autumn the foliage gradually turns to glossy yellow, then gold and orange. Finally, in a good year, the whole tree is flaming red and crimson, appearing to light up everything around.

The inconspicuous, small, green, early-summer flowers are followed by equally disappointing small, blue fruit. The tupelo will tolerate a moist, well-drained, acid soil but may suffer if the soil dries out for a period. Although hardy, it dislikes cold winds, and will colour better after a hot summer. It does not transplant well and will succeed best if planted as a small tree. In Britain it is usually grown as a multi-stemmed tree with a height of 20m (66ft) and a spread of 10m (33ft). The variety 'Sheffield Park' colours to a brilliant orange-red at least three weeks before *N. sylvatica*.

Olea europaea
OLIVE

If you can grow and fruit an olive you are in the Mediterranean basin. So the story goes. They grow well in California, too, so that knocks that theory on the head. My tree manages to survive in a pot, providing I mollycoddle it in a sheltered corner all winter and spring. Even so, I'm sure the temperature rises and the sun shines when I approach it.

The evergreen 7.5cm (3in) long, leathery leaves are grey-green on the upper side and silvery-green on the underside. Panicles of small, creamy-white, fragrant flowers 5cm (2in) long appear in summer followed by 2.5cm (1in) green olives, which ripen to black. Eating olives are harvested either half or fully ripe. When grown for oil, the fruit is left on the tree until fully ripe.

Olive trees are slow-growing, living for hundreds of years and becoming gnarled and misshapen. The wood is hard with a close grain and is ideal for carving. They need an open, well-drained soil with added grit, in full sun with shelter from

above
OLEA EUROPAEA
needs a lot of tender loving care in anything but the mildest of climates – but the results are worth the effort.

cold winds. Olives hate humidity. In my locality the best chance of needing to buy an olive oil press is to plant a young tree on a warm, sunny wall under the eaves of the roof to keep off most of the rain. In Britain, given ideal conditions, it will grow to a height and spread of 9m (30ft).

Osmanthus yunnanensis

An excellent choice of tree for winter fragrance. The 20cm (8in) long, evergreen leaves are a glossy, dark green. On the same plant some of the leaves will be spiny toothed while others remain smooth. The small tubular creamy-white flowers are very fragrant and appear in clusters during late winter and early spring. The smallest spray of flowers is sufficient to perfume a room. They are followed by small, deep purple fruit covered in a white bloom.

The tree is fully hardy but enjoys a sheltered site protected from cold winds. It will grow well in most soils except wet, poorly drained ground. Pruning may be necessary to encourage it to form a tree shape rather than a multi-stemmed plant. At maturity it will have a height and spread of 9m (30ft).

Ostyra carpinifolia
HOP HORNBEAM

The dark-green, deciduous, 10cm (4in) leaves are double-toothed, turning brilliant golden yellow in autumn. This display is not dependent on soil or on having a good season. The male catkins are bright yellow and pendulous, forming in autumn and opening in spring, while the female flowers are upright. Clusters of hop-like fruit are white in summer, turning brown in autumn, when they show well against the yellow leaves.

This tree makes no demands, tolerating
most soils except those which are very
wet. It is hardy, succeeding in sun or
shade. The species O. *virginiana*
(American hop hornbeam) is more
frequently grown in American gardens.
The two are similar, although O. *virginiana*
makes a smaller more conical tree. The
hop hornbeam will grow to a height of
20m (66ft) with a spread of 15m (50ft).

Parrotia persica

PERSIAN IRONWOOD

A small deciduous tree. I have never seen
a specimen the shape of which I would
have been proud. Generally they form a
spreading bush with tiers of horizontal
branches heading in every direction. The
13cm (5in) long glossy green leaves have
the ability to turn to yellow, orange and
red in autumn. Some years the display is a
bit hit or miss, with the first leaves to
colour falling before the remainder turn.

When mature the grey and fawn bark
peels in long strips. Flowering in winter in
dense clusters along the branches, the
petalless flowers have bright red stamens
but are subject to frost damage.

It prefers a well-drained, fertile soil in sun
or light shade. There is a better chance of
good autumn leaf colour when it is grown in
an acid soil. It will reach a height of 8m
(26ft) with a spread of 10m (33ft).

Paulownia tomentosa

FOXGLOVE TREE, EMPRESS TREE

The tree is deciduous with large,
30cm (12in), bright, light green leaves,
hairy on both surfaces. The flowers form in
the autumn and overwinter as buds, which
is bad news for gardeners who experience
hard frosts every winter. For the past 12

PARROTIA PERSICA
In a good year on acid soil the leaves will
make a marvellous autumn display.

years I have been excited at the first sight
of flower buds and the prospect of spring
flowers on my tree. On only four occasions
has my wish come true. I still consider it
worth the many disappointments to see
the display when it happens. The flowers
appear as upright spikes of foxglove-
shaped, violet-scented, purple-lilac blooms
with purple and yellow marks on the
inside. The oval capsules that follow hold
winged seed.

If you tire of waiting for a frost-free
spring, coppice the tree in late spring,

cutting the pithy stems to 30cm (12in) from the ground. Thick, strong shoots will grow to 3m (10ft), well clothed with extra large, softly hairy, ornamental leaves. Repeat annually for a leafy show.

Paulownia tomentosa is perfectly hardy, although young plants may be damaged by frost. Plant in a well drained, fertile site in full sun. It quickly forms a tree 11m (36ft) in height with a spread of 8m (26ft).

Photinia davidiana

Of all the photinias this is the most likely to perform well in cooler climates with a good show of flower and fruit. Previously it was named *Stranvaesia davidiana*, so you may still come across it under this name. The leathery, evergreen 12.5cm (5in) long, lance-shaped leaves are dark green. Older leaves turn deep red in late autumn. In summer, panicles of small white flowers up to 7.5cm (3in) across appear, followed by pendant clusters of small, bright red fruit on red-brown stalks. There is a variety *P. d.* var. *undulata* 'Fructu Luteo' with bright yellow fruit. 'Palette', another variety, has foliage blotched and splashed with cream and pink and, in my opinion, is the most awful plant ever to come out of Holland. Fortunately it is slow-growing.

Photinia is not particular regarding soil type but prefers a well-drained soil in a sunny site sheltered from cold winds. It is tolerant of an alkaline soil. Fire blight disease can be a problem and may in time cause the death of the tree. A shrubby habit is natural with many stiff ascending branches. Allowing one leader to grow away will ensure a tree with a good trunk to a height of 8m (26ft) and spreading to 5m (16ft).

PAULOWNIA TOMENTOSA
with its interesting, foxglove-like spring flowers. It dislikes cold winter winds as the flower buds are produced in the late autumn.

Populus alba

WHITE POPLAR, ABELE

There are four types of poplar: black, white, balsam and trembling. White poplars have white undersides to the leaf. The deciduous, five-lobed, 10cm (4in) long, maple-like leaves emerge on white, hairy, young shoots. They are dark green on the upper surface. In autumn the upper surface turns to buttercup yellow, or red in America.

Allowed to grow unchecked, a tree will become straggly and tend to lean away from the slightest breeze. It responds well to hard pruning to keep it in shape, otherwise it will grow to a height of 30m (100ft) with a spread of 15m (50ft). Suckering into lawns and elsewhere may be a nuisance: if the suckers are allowed to grow, they soon form a thicket.

This poplar can tolerate most soil conditions, except ground which is constantly waterlogged; it will succeed well on dry, impoverished soil, making a good windbreak in coastal areas. There are two varieties of interest: 'Richardii' is slower growing, making a smaller tree, and the upper surface of its leaves is yellow instead of green, making it attractive against a dark background; *P. a. f. pyramidalis* has an upright habit with erect branches resembling the Lombardy poplar, *P. nigra* 'Italica' (see opposite), but broader at the base.

Populus x candicans 'Aurora'

VARIEGATED BALM OF GILEAD, VARIEGATED ONTARIO POPLAR

Sometimes found in books listed under *P. x. jackii* 'Aurora' this female variety is, unfortunately, prone to bacterial canker and is usually short-lived. I have to declare an interest and admit that I hate the sight

above
POPULUS ALBA
Where there is space for a large tree, the white poplar quickly fills it.

right
POPULUS TREMULA 'PENDULA'
The male catkins of the aspen appear with the snowdrops in late winter and are every bit as welcome.

of this tree, especially in a rural setting. When it is growing well it is gaudy and when poorly grown it looks miserable. The deciduous leaves are heart-shaped at the base and 15cm (6in) long. They open mid-green with cream, white and pink splashes. As they age the pink disappears. Some leaves will be completely creamy-yellow, while leaves towards the centre of the tree will be green.

Pruning the side stems hard every winter will encourage strong new shoots with larger leaves and more variegation. It

is worth noting that frequently in the first year after planting the tree does not produce any variegation. Don't dig it up and complain, just be patient.

Most soil types are suitable with the exception of waterlogged ground or very dry conditions. 'Aurora' is totally hardy but strong winds may damage the foliage, causing it to turn brown prematurely. It will form a large dome-headed tree 13m (43ft) in height with a spread of 6m (20ft).

Populus nigra 'Italica'
LOMBARDY POPLAR

Love it or hate it, this tall, narrow, columnar, anorexic-looking tree has changed the view of landscapes across Europe. Lombardy poplars march kilometre after kilometre along both sides of Napoleon's French roads. Towering up out of deep valleys in the Alps, they emphasise the height of the surrounding mountains. On flat farmland, boundaries can be seen when the fields themselves are lost in haze. Thin upright branches cling to the main stem from the base up. The deciduous, glossy green leaves are 10cm (4in) long and turn yellow and then brown in autumn. It is a male tree, brought to Essex in England from Turin in Italy in 1758 and now common throughout the British Isles.

It is not fussy regarding soil but will be faster-growing in a deep fertile soil that is well drained. Totally hardy, it makes an effective, quick-growing windbreak and screen but it is prone to bacterial canker.

At maturity it will reach a height of 30m (100ft) spreading to 4m (13ft). The variety 'Plantierensis' makes a slightly broader tree and is commonly planted instead of 'Italica'.

'Lombardy Gold' is an attractive golden-leaved sport discovered on a mature Lombardy poplar in Surrey, England.

Populus tremula 'Pendula'
WEEPING ASPEN,
TREMBLING POPLAR

Aspen leaves are always on the move. Even when there isn't a breath of air they shiver and shake. The secret lies in the long, thin leaf stalk held at right angles to the dangling leaf blade. The ultimate in privacy and pleasure is to picnic under a weeping aspen and listen to its constant whispering.

It is a formidable suckering tree and it is said that after Napoleon reduced most of Moscow to ashes in 1813, the common aspen (P. tremula) colonized the ruins.

The deciduous, rough toothed, 7.5cm (3in) long leaves are bronze when they first open, turning a dark green in summer and bright yellow in autumn. The tree is male, producing grey-red catkins 7.5cm (3in) long in early spring. It will grow quickly in a well-drained, moist soil in a sunny situation, making a well-shaped, weeping tree with a height and spread of 7m (23ft).

Prunus

THE CHERRY FAMILY FORMS A LARGE AND diverse group of trees with evergreen and deciduous species, both ornamental and fruiting. Ornamental cherries include the Japanese flowering cherries which, like daffodils, remind us that winter is over.

Ornamental cherries have more than their share of diseases, some of which may be fatal. They are particularly prone to silver leaf disease, where the fungus spores enter through a wound. If it is necessary to shape the tree by pruning, carry out the work in summer when the disease is dormant. A plant care label could reasonably read 'don't prunus in winter'.

Cherries are easy to grow on any reasonably fertile soil, acid or limy, providing it is free-draining with no risk of waterlogging. They are hardy but prefer to grow in a sunny situation. Strong winds during flowering will destroy the show, leaving the ground carpeted with petals like confetti.

They have a shallow root system and some of the roots have a bad habit of rising to ground level, damaging hard surfaces and lawns. Removing the occasional troublesome surface root from a mature tree will not set it back or weaken it. Cherries, like crab apples, are good value for money with bonus points for flower, attractive bark and autumn leaf colour.

Prunus 'Accolade'

This hybrid cherry with *P. sargentii* and *P.* x *subhirtella* as parents is deserving of its name. The deciduous leaves are thin, 10cm (4in) long and dark green. They seem to be in short supply, giving the tree a sparse appearance. In autumn the foliage turns to orange-red, hanging on until the first frost or strong wind. Masses of pendulous clusters of semi-double, rich

Prunus 'Amanogawa'
ORNAMENTAL JAPANESE CHERRY

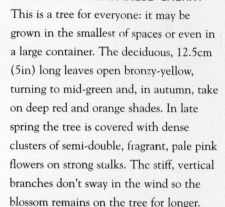

This is a tree for everyone: it may be grown in the smallest of spaces or even in a large container. The deciduous, 12.5cm (5in) long leaves open bronzy-yellow, turning to mid-green and, in autumn, take on deep red and orange shades. In late spring the tree is covered with dense clusters of semi-double, fragrant, pale pink flowers on strong stalks. The stiff, vertical branches don't sway in the wind so the blossom remains on the tree for longer.

It prefers a moist, well-drained, fertile soil with added compost in a sunny site. This multi-stemmed, slim, columnar tree grows to a height of 7m (23ft) with a total spread, after a long time, of 3m (10ft).

Prunus 'Cheal's Weeping'
WEEPING ORNAMENTAL CHERRY

Sometimes wrongly labelled *P.* 'Kiku-shidare-zakura', this is a very manageable small weeping cherry tree which is perfectly behaved. But just occasionally it will send out a sucker, close to, but below, the graft. Left unnoticed it will quickly head for heaven, usurping the weaker variety, leaving you with a larger-than-life, white-flowered wild cherry (*P. avium*).

The young, 10cm (4in) long, deciduous leaves are bronze-green, turning to a glossy mid-green. There is seldom any autumn colour. Flowers appear in early spring before, or at the same time as, the leaves. They are bright clear pink and double, up to 2.5cm (1in) in diameter, and held in clusters on every branch.

Arching branches that reach the ground will continue to grow horizontally if not summer-pruned to reduce the length. Grown in a tall container, the flowering

PRUNUS 'CHEAL'S WEEPING'
is a good early-spring flowering cherry with double clear pink flowers.

pink flowers open in spring from deep pink buds. The clusters are made up of three flowers, each 2.5cm (1in) across with frilled petals.

It prefers a moist, well-drained, fertile soil in full sun with shelter from strong winds at blossom time. 'Accolade' forms a medium-sized tree with an open, straggly head. It will mature to a height and spread of 8m (26ft).

stems have further to descend, resulting in a better display. The weeping cherry prefers full sun in a moist, well-drained soil. Avoid planting in a lawn, as grass maintenance is difficult. It will grow to a height of 3m (10ft) with a similar spread.

Prunus 'Kanzan'

ORNAMENTAL FLOWERING JAPANESE CHERRY

This tree is sometimes incorrectly labelled *P.* 'Kwanzan'. Most gardeners either love or hate this tree, but I can not make up my mind. It is very common and the flowers are a funny colour pink. I have one in my garden so that says something, but would I plant another one? It's enormous, it flowers untidily and the blossom is a difficult colour.

The large, deciduous 12.5cm (5in) long dark green leaves open a deep bronze when young. At best they display some yellow in autumn. The short-lived flowers are easily recognised. Anything but cherry in colour, they appear in mid- to late spring, fully double at 5cm (2in) across, in a deep, dusky, mauve-pink. They grow in clusters of two to five flowers at the same time as or before the leaves appear. After five to seven days the petals litter the lawn, patio and flower beds like confetti, before turning a dull brown and becoming a nuisance.

On the plus side, there is no such thing as an off year for flowering with 'Kanzan'. It never fails to give 100 per cent bloom, irrespective of weather conditions.

Plant in a sunny site in a moist, well-drained soil. Its habit of spreading some of its roots at soil level rules it out for planting in a lawn. If it can be sited in front of a large dark conifer or building it

PRUNUS 'KANZAN'
This is how I like to remember 'Kanzan', with bronze young foliage and the emerging flowers still delicate.

will look less startlingly pink in bloom. Planted on a height with blue sky behind it is memorable in flower and is easily forgiven its little whims. Of course I would plant another one.

As a young tree the branches are ascending, giving the tree a vase-like shape that appears to be ideal for planting

in streets or confined spaces.
Unfortunately, it grows out of this habit,
turning into a large, spreading tree with a
mature height and spread of 10m (33ft).

Prunus lusitanica
PORTUGAL LAUREL

It's not a cherry tree and it's not really a
laurel, but it is from Portugal. The
evergreen 13cm (5in) glossy, dark green
leaves are held on red stalks and make a
good backdrop for the small, cup-shaped
white flowers in summer. The 25cm (10in)
racemes of flowers are sweet-smelling and
are followed by small cherry-like, deep red
fruit that ripen to purple-black. Game birds
such as pheasants and grouse love the fruit
and the cover the tree provides. It will
establish on the poorest of soils and can
tolerate dry, alkaline, conditions. Hardy in
all but the coldest areas of Britain, it enjoys
a site in sun or partial shade.

Cherry laurel may be planted to form a
screen, making a dense evergreen hedge
that can be clipped into shape in late
summer after flowering. When mature it
forms a large, many-branched tree, 20m
(66ft) high with a spread of 15m (50ft).

Prunus padus 'Watereri'
BIRD CHERRY

'Watereri' is a selected form of the English
bird cherry P. padus and much better all
round. The bark of young branches is a
shiny, smooth dark brown that glistens
when wet. Its deciduous, 10cm (4 in)
long, dark green leaves turn yellow and
sometimes red in late autumn. Individual
flowers are tiny but are massed as fragrant,
white, 20cm (8in) long pendant racemes
in late spring. They are followed, in
autumn, by small, glossy, black fruits,

PRUNUS SARGENTII
is a 'must have' cherry where space allows.
The blossom is great, but autumn leaf
colour is magnificent – and see page 47 for
a glimpse of its lustrous mahogany-
coloured bark.

which will be devoured by birds, especially
blackbirds, almost before they are ripe.

This tree will succeed in the worst of soils
providing there is adequate moisture. It
tolerates alkaline and impoverished ground.
It is totally hardy and the early spring flower
show is not affected by wind. In a sunny
garden situation it will grow to 15m (50ft)
high with a spread of 10m (33ft).

There are other varieties worth growing:
'Colorata' has dark purple shoots, crimson-
purple young foliage and small icing-sugar
pink flowers; 'Albertii' is more upright
with stiff branches and short, erect
racemes of flowers.

Prunus sargentii
SARGENT'S CHERRY

This has to be one of the best of the
cherries. It is deciduous and will reach a
height and spread of 15m (50ft). In spring,
before the leaves appear, the tree is
covered in single, icing-sugar pink flowers.

Just before the blossom falls, the young, copper-bronze leaves appear, creating a startling effect. In summer the leaves turn dark green. By late summer the 12.5cm (5in) long leaves start to droop and suddenly turn brilliant red and orange, long before other trees have realised it is autumn. The small, shiny, deep crimson fruit hang well into winter.

The bark is a lustrous, dark mahogany, evident even on the young branches; it shines on a wet winter's day like chestnuts fresh from their shells. The trunk has a habit of forking low down. If the plant is small, cut one of the leaders in early summer, allowing the remaining stem to grow straight without the risk of a narrow angle forming between the two trunks and eventually splitting. This is the only cherry tree the bullfinches leave alone in my garden. All the others suffer bud loss before the end of winter.

Prunus 'Spire'

Hillier's catalogue claims this tree to be 'probably the best small street tree raised last century'. They should know, it was raised in their nursery and used to be labelled *P.* x *hillieri* 'Spire'. I have no problem agreeing with the statement and would add that it makes a wonderful tree for any but the smallest garden.

The 10cm (4in) long, deciduous leaves are bronze when young, turning dark green in summer before taking on beautiful autumn orange, gold and red tints. The bowl-shaped, single, pale, soft orchid-pink flowers appear in mid-spring at the same time as the young, bronze foliage. They hang in clusters of three to five all along the ascending branches. 'Spire' will grow in most soils with the exception of waterlogged ground. It prefers an open site in full sun. The tree is conical when young, becoming vase-shaped as it ages, and growing to a height of 10m (33ft) with a spread of 6m (20ft).

Prunus x subhirtella 'Autumnalis'
WINTER-FLOWERING CHERRY, ROSEBUD CHERRY

A cherry to gladden your heart on a dull, cold, miserable, winter's day. It is deciduous with 7.5cm (3in) long, dark green, sharply toothed leaves. They open bronze-green turning to gold in autumn. Small, semi-double flowers open white from pink buds and appear in late autumn. It will continue to flower, during mild periods, throughout the winter until spring. When the weather is cold the flower buds refuse to open, hanging on short stalks close to the main stems, until it turns milder. There is seldom a prolonged period over winter when the tree is without flower. Seen at dusk or against a watery-blue sky it is spectacular in flower.

It prefers a moist, fertile, well-drained soil in full sun but sheltered from cold winter winds. The crown is open in habit. It will grow to 8m (26ft) high with a spread of 7m (23ft). The variety 'Autumnalis Rosea' has the same habit of growth but with small shell-pink flowers.

left
PRUNUS 'SPIRE'
is upright in habit, so needs less space than most cherries.

right
PRUNUS X SUBHIRTELLA 'AUTUMNALIS'
As well as flowering with the spring bulbs, it produces some flowers from autumn onwards.

Pyrus salicifolia 'Pendula'

WEEPING SILVER PEAR

This deciduous pear tree does not really weep as one would imagine it. The branches spread out and up, but the tips hang down, giving the appearance of weeping, although the mature tree itself is really more of a shaggy, tousled, pendulous shape.

The 7.5cm (3in) long, willow-like leaves are silvery-grey when young, changing to silver-green as they age. Creamy-white flowers appear in spring in clusters of six to eight, followed in autumn by small, green, 2.5cm (1in) fruit. Shaped like an inverted pear, they ripen to dark brown but are inedible.

Its pendulous habit will be improved by summer pruning to remove some of the crossing and tangled branches. Tipping back – removing up to one third of the growth of vigorous shoots that are heading out instead of down – enhances the overall shape.

The foliage may suffer badly from regular attacks of rust. In severe cases the plant is defoliated, sending out a second flush of clean leaves the same summer. It prefers a well-drained, moist, fertile soil in full sun and will grow to 5m (16ft) high with a spread of 4m (13ft).

PYRUS SALICIFOLIA 'PENDULA' is grown mainly for its leaf and its weeping habit. The creamy-white flowers are a bonus.

Quercus ilex

EVERGREEN OAK, HOLM OAK, HOLLY OAK

Holm is the old English word for holly, thus the tree's botanical name of *ilex*, the Latin for holly. This tree is the biggest of all the broadleaf, evergreen trees in the northern hemisphere.

The grey bark eventually becomes black and rugged, with cracks dividing the surface into small squares. The 7.5cm (3in) or smaller, glossy, dark green, leathery leaves are pale silvery-green on the underside. New, pale amber-green leaves are produced on white, woolly shoots in summer at the same time as small, yellow catkins. The shape and size of the leaves varies considerably and depends on the age of the tree and the growing conditions. Small grey-green, almost round acorns are produced in clumps of two or three in autumn.

left

QUERCUS ILEX
produces masses of catkins at the same time as the new leaves. See page 110 for this tree in all its glory, and page 114 for the acorns.

below

QUERCUS PALUSTRIS
After a long hot summer the autumn colour is wonderful.

branches fanning out to form a domed head, while the lower branches sweep down to ground level.

The deeply cut, seven-lobed, deciduous, mid-green leaves are 15cm (6in) long and carry large tufts of pale brown hairs at the vein axils on the underside. In autumn the leaves turn scarlet before falling.

This tree will tolerate a dry soil, but prefers a wet site. Plant it in full sun in a sheltered situation, protected from cold winds. It will grow to 20m (66ft) high with a spread of 10m (33ft).

This tree prefers a rich, well-drained, fertile soil in a sunny site although it can tolerate heavy shade. It is a good tree for coastal planting, making a fine, evergreen, clipped hedge, immune to salt deposits on its foliage. Inland, it may be prone to leaf damage from cold spring winds. A mature tree is a majestic sight, 25m (80ft) high and spreading to over 20m (66ft).

Quercus palustris
PIN OAK

In Britain this oak is suitable only for the south and west, where there is the chance of a good summer. In eastern parts of North America it grows beautifully, making a large tree. It grows quickly for a few years, then settles down to a moderate rate of growth. The overall shape is unusual for an oak, with lots of thin

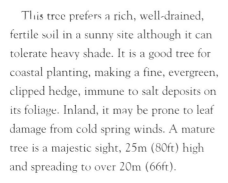

Other notable oaks include:

Quercus cerris

TURKEY OAK

A large, deciduous, fast-growing tree that tolerates alkaline soil and maritime sites. Its dark green leaves turn yellow-brown in autumn. It grows to a height of 30m (100ft) with a spread of 25m (80ft).

Quercus petraea

SESSILE OAK

A spreading tree with deciduous, dark green, yellow-stalked leaves with rounded lobes. It grows to a height of 30m (100ft) with a spread of 25m (80ft).

Quercus robur

COMMON OAK, ENGLISH OAK, PEDUNCULATE OAK

A large, deciduous tree with dark green leaves with rounded lobes. The base of each leaf has two small matching lobes. It grows to a height of 35m (116ft) with a spread of 25m (80ft). The variety 'Concordia' or golden oak is smaller and slow-growing with golden yellow leaves in spring and early summer, turning pale green in autumn before falling. 'Strypemonde' produces narrow, sharply lobed leaves that are mottled bright yellow.

Quercus rubra

RED OAK

A fast-growing, deciduous tree with dark green leaves up to 20cm (8in) long with sharp-pointed lobes. The leaves turn to brilliant shades of yellow, orange, red and brown in autumn. The red oak succeeds best on an acid soil and grows to a height of 25m (80ft) with a spread of 18m (60ft).

Rhamnus cathartica

COMMON BUCKTHORN

More usually grown as a shrub, this plant will, if shaped, form a substantial, deciduous, spiny tree. The glossy, 5cm (2in) long, dark green leaves turn a mellow yellow in autumn and persist for a long period. In late spring and early summer small, yellow-green clusters of flowers form in the leaf axils. They are followed, in autumn, by clusters of spherical, red fruit which ripen to black and contrast with the autumn leaf colour. Buckthorn will grow in most soils but prefers moist ground that doesn't dry out

far left
QUERCUS ROBUR
is the archetypal English oak – a majestic, spreading tree if you have the space for it.

left
QUERCUS RUBRA
has some of the best autumn colour of all the oaks.

below
RHODODENDRON ARBORFUM
will grow to 11m (33ft) in height given the right conditions, and may produce red, pink or white flowers.

The evergreen, 20cm (8in) long leaves are dark green on the upper side. The underside is covered in indumentum, which may be orange-brown, fawn or silver. In early spring large trusses of bell-shaped flowers, 5cm (2in) long appear. The flowers may be white, pink or red, each with black spots on the inside.

Plant the tree in a deep, moist, fertile, well-drained, acid soil with lots of added leaf mould. It prefers a sheltered, shaded site in a woodland situation where it will grow to a height of 11m (36ft) with a spread of 4m (13ft). There are many varieties of R. *arboreum* worth growing but for hardy trees in a range of colours I would plant 'Album' with large white flowers, R. *a.* var. *roseum* for its deep pink flowers with dark spots and 'Blood Red', which has deep, dark red flowers early in the spring.

in summer. It enjoys an alkaline soil in sun or partial shade. Early pruning to reduce the side shoots and form a main stem will allow the plant to produce an open, dome-headed tree that will grow to a height of 6m (20ft) with a spread of 5m (16ft).

Rhododendron arboreum

TREE RHODODENDRON

This species of rhododendron was the first to be brought to Britain from the Himalayas as seed in 1820. It is the forerunner of many of our finest hardy hybrids and introduced deep crimson-red to strengthen the paler flower colours that preceded it. It wasn't hardy enough for outdoors and spent its early years in conservatories, but its hybrid progeny proved to be much tougher.

Rhododendron macabeanum

There are those who would class this magnificent plant as a shrub and I wouldn't argue with them but I'd point out that, if so, it grows to be a very large shrub. On his expedition to India and Burma in 1927, Frank Kingdon Ward describes it in his field notes as 'a forest tree with handsome foliage . . . it goes right to the summit where it forms forests'. That gives it the pedigree to be listed in this book.

The evergreen, 30cm (12in) long leaves are glossy, dark green on the upper side with noticeable veins. The underside is covered with a grey-white tomentum. In early spring it displays masses of large trusses of pale yellow flowers with purple blotches. On the occasional plant the flowers may be a deep orange-yellow. Each truss may carry as many as 20 bell-shaped flowers.

This tree prefers a shaded woodland site, sheltered from cold spring winds. A deep, fertile, moist, well-drained, acid soil is ideal. It can tolerate hard pruning, growing away again even from large stumps. At maturity it will have a height of 15m (50ft) with a spread of 5m (16ft).

Robinia pseudoacacia 'Frisia'
FALSE ACACIA, LOCUST

The parent plant *R. pseudoacacia* produces long, black, bean-like seed pods. Settlers in America assumed these were the 'locusts' on which John the Baptist fed in the wilderness. I don't think so, especially as this tree is native only to America. In England, it is called acacia as its leaves vaguely resemble this plant, hence its Latin name *pseudoacacia* or 'false acacia'. It has pairs of sharp spines on the young wood

above
ROBINIA PSEUDOACACIA 'FRISIA'
For golden deciduous foliage this is as good as you could wish for.

right
SALIX BABYLONICA VAR. PEKINENSIS 'TORTUOSA'
I enjoy trying to trace the route of a single bare branch against a sullen grey sky.

and some are retained on the old wood, making it dangerous for children to climb.

The deciduous, pinnate 30cm (12in) long leaves are made up of 20-23 leaflets opening butter-yellow in the late spring. As they age they become a pale yellow with a green tint. In autumn the yellow turns to orange before falling at the first suggestion of frost. I have never seen 'Frisia' in flower but its parent species flowers well in a hot, dry season with masses of fragrant, small white flowers during early summer.

Robinias love a fertile, well-drained soil in full sun but will tolerate impoverished, dry, stony ground. They are hardy, except in the coldest areas of Britain, but their brittle branches mean they need to be planted in a site sheltered from strong winds. 'Frisia' is prone to throw suckers at the base. Unfortunately, since it is grafted, they are green-leaved like the parent species. At maturity, it may have a height of 14m (46ft) with a spread of 6m (20ft).

Salix alba subsp. vitellina 'Britzensis'

RED-STEMMED WILLOW

At the time of writing I think I have got the name correct. Somebody, or perhaps more than one person, keeps changing it. You may know the tree as *Salix alba* 'Britzensis' or various other names, but it is the one with the orange-red winter bark. The deciduous, 10cm (4in) long, dull, mid-green leaves are blue-green on the underside. In spring yellow, 5cm (2in) long, male catkins are produced at the same time as the leaves.

The real show comes in winter when the bare stems display their coloured bark. The younger branches have the most colour, especially the current year's growths. There is a temptation to coppice this tree annually in spring, cutting it close to the ground to encourage a mass of young, brightly coloured stems. I can't disagree with the practice but the result is a striking shrub for winter colour, rather than a tree. Stay your hand and have patience. All the time the tree is growing well and making lots of new growth, it will put on its orange-red winter cloak. On a mature tree the effect is like a great cloud of orange smoke.

It prefers to be planted in a moist, well-drained, fertile soil in full sun but can

tolerate having its feet close to water. Growth is poor in very wet soil or in shallow soil over chalk. It will grow to a height of 20m (66ft) with a spread of 10m (33ft).

Salix babylonica var. pekinensis 'Tortuosa'

DRAGON'S CLAW WILLOW, CORKSCREW WILLOW

Stopping short of being a mere curiosity, 'Tortuosa' forms an elegant garden tree. Every young stem on the tree is contorted with spirals and bends, sending branches in a dozen different directions. As the tree ages the main stem and older branches tend to straighten, losing the more severe manic twists. The contortions are also less noticeable when the tree is in leaf. The deciduous leaves appear early in spring and are bright green, fading to pale green in summer before turning yellow in late autumn. They are twisted and curled as though suffering from a pest such as a sucking insect. Insignificant green-yellow female catkins appear in spring at the same time as the leaves.

As a young tree 'Tortuosa' is very fast-growing but tends to slow down after a few years.

It can look awkward and top heavy when it is grown as a standard tree with 2m (6ft 6in) of clean trunk. Allowing it to branch at 1m (3ft) above ground improves its appearance.

This willow prefers a deep, fertile soil. It will tolerate wet ground providing it is not waterlogged. It dislikes an alkaline soil. Plant it in a sunny situation, sheltered from strong winds. Pruning by removing branches for indoor decoration will encourage new growth. It will grow to a height of 15m (50ft) with a spread of 8m (26ft).

Salix caprea 'Kilmarnock'
WEEPING KILMARNOCK WILLOW

If you haven't room for this tree you really are short of space. It will even grow quite happily for years in a large container. The pendulous stems are orange-brown and quickly build up to form a congested head. The older stems form a lower layer that soon dies off. If they are not pruned out, the new branches form layer after layer on top, eventually making a large spreading head. When purchasing a tree, select one

right
SOPHORA TETRAPTERA
bears deep orange-yellow flowers that give way to interesting seed pods. With tender loving care it will produce masses of seed pods.

where the graft has been made as high as possible so that it forms a tall specimen.

The deciduous, 10cm (4in) long, toothed leaves are dark green on the upper surface and grey-green on the underside. Male catkins appear before the foliage in late winter and early spring. They are silvery, opening to display golden anthers.

This willow loves a well-drained, fertile soil in full sun. Although it never grows to be a large tree, it has a weak, confined root system and will probably need to be permanently staked and tied. Remember to check regularly that the tie isn't tight and cutting into the bark. It makes a compact tree and its height depends on the position of the graft: 2m (6ft 6in) is typical, with the same spread. There is a female variety, 'Weeping Sally', which is more vigorous but the catkins are smaller and less attractive.

Sophora japonica
JAPANESE PAGODA TREE

A native of China, this beautiful, deciduous tree nevertheless does have a Japanese look to it. The first pagoda tree in Britain was planted in 1762 in Kew Gardens, London and it can still be seen today. It is like an enormous 'step-over' with its main trunk reclining parallel to the ground, supported on props. Perhaps it got tired waiting to flower.

The deciduous, 30cm (12in) long, pinnate leaves are made up of 9-15 leaflets. They are glossy dark green, turning golden yellow in late autumn. The flowers are small, creamy-white and fragrant and appear in late summer in large, 30cm (12in) long, terminal panicles. The pea-like seed pods are bright green ageing to yellow and, as the seed swells, the pod resembles a string of pale green beads. When grown in a sheltered site the pods will hang on the tree until spring.

This tree needs long, hot, dry summers to encourage it to flower and even then only mature trees will bloom. Perhaps 'Chinese patience tree' would be a better name. It will succeed best if planted in a well-drained soil, in full sun, in a site protected from cold winds, where it can grow to a height of 30m (100ft) with a spread of 15m (50ft).

The variety 'Violacea' has the same habit of growth with white flowers tinged with deep pink. It is every bit as slow to produce them.

Sophora tetraptera

KOWHAI

Sometimes called the New Zealand laburnum, this tree is the national flower of that country. It is not fully hardy and while evergreen in warmer climates, in nearly all areas of Britain it is deciduous. Given a little pampering it will survive most winters.

The branches tend to spread or droop and grow in a zigzag habit. The pinnate, 18cm (7in) long, grey-green leaves comprise up to 40 leaflets. In late spring the pea-shaped, 5cm (2in) long, tubular, deep golden-yellow flowers appear in drooping clusters. They are followed in autumn by peculiar-looking beaded seed pods, each with four broad wings.

Plant it in a sheltered, warm corner or against a sunny wall. It dislikes transplanting and needs to be planted as a small tree in a well-drained, fertile soil. Prune only when absolutely necessary. It will grow to a height of 10m (33ft) with a spread of 4m (13ft).

Sorbus

ROWAN TREE, MOUNTAIN ASH AND WHITE-beam are familiar members of a group of trees that thrive in cooler climes. There are two types of sorbus that differ only in leaf shape. The rowan or mountain ash (*Sorbus aucuparia*) has deciduous, compound leaves with up to 30 leaflets per leaf rather like an ash (*Fraxinus*). Whitebeam (*S. aria*) leaves are deciduous, single, simple, sometimes lobed or more usually toothed. Frequently the underside is white felted.

It has to be said that you are unlikely to plant any sorbus for its flowers. They do have them – sometimes enormous heads of tiny, off-white or cream flowers – but they are usually hidden by the foliage. What they lack in flowers they make up for in berries. In late summer and autumn those dull flowers are transformed into berries in bunches that are heavy enough to bend branches. Depending on species or variety, they may be white, yellow, orange, pink or brilliant red.

Foliage interest depends on the season. The mountain ash tends to come into its own with autumn colour, while whitebeam foliage is at its glorious best as the new leaves unfurl in the spring. The leaves uncurl in an upright position like a candle with the undersides silky, chalk white. On a breezy sunny day the whole plant shimmers like a flock of white doves. In summer they lose their charm but interest is revived in autumn when they turn russet-brown.

Sorbus are tolerant of most soils and climates but prefer a moist, well-drained soil. Whitebeam will succeed on alkaline or acid sites. Mountain ash and its varieties enjoy an acid to neutral soil type.

Sorbus aria 'Lutescens'
WHITEBEAM

All of the sorbus give value for money and 'Lutescens' is at its best in spring and again in autumn. The deciduous, young leaves are almost pure white when they open. When the 12cm (5in) long simple leaf is fully open, the upper surface is silvery-white turning to sea-green in summer. The underside is pure white. In autumn the foliage turns to amber and russet – a backdrop for the large clusters of bright scarlet berries. The fruit ripens early, turning from green through pale brown to red in a few weeks.

Whitebeam will grow in most soils, including alkaline and dry ground. It prefers a deep, moist, well-drained, fertile site in sun or partial shade, where it will grow to 10m (33ft) with a spread of 7m (23ft).

Sorbus aucuparia

ROWAN, MOUNTAIN ASH

Beautiful leaves, flowers and fruit provide some of the reasons for wanting a rowan in the garden. If you can't justify the space for any of the usual reasons then plant one for peace of mind. Since the begining of time the rowan has been used for good luck, good health and to ward off evil spirits. A sprig, small branch or a small cross made of the wood was considered sufficient protection. To own a whole tree, growing close to your house, is the equivalent of fully comprehensive cover.

The large, 20cm (8in) long, deciduous, mid-green pinnate leaves have up to 12 sharply toothed leaflets. In early autumn they turn to brilliant shades of yellow, orange and bright red. Clusters of white flowers appear in late spring and are

followed by large bunches of small, orange-red berries. The fruit is rich in vitamin C and pectin. Birds love the berries and until recently, in some parts of Europe, they were used as bait to catch birds for the pot. A better use is in the making of a glorious, deep orange jelly with an interesting bittersweet flavour, ideal with game.

It will succeed in most soils but prefers a light, sandy, well-drained, acid soil in full sun or shade. When planted in a wet loam or peat soil it prefers to be in full sun. On an alkaline soil the head of the tree tends to open up, becoming sparse with branches dying out, and is often short-lived. A native tree, it is totally hardy throughout the northern hemisphere as far north as Iceland. In the British Isles it will grow to 15m (50ft) with a spread of 7m (23ft).

The variety 'Fructu Luteo' differs in its bright amber-yellow fruit. It quickly forms a spreading tree, the masses of fruit appearing to form a yellow cloud when viewed from a distance in the autumn. Birds usually leave the fruit untouched until they are starving and have eaten all the red berries in the garden. Like all the other varieties of S. *aucuparia* it is fast growing and may be transplanted as a large specimen. It will grow to a height of 8m (26ft) with a spread of 6m (20ft).

below
SORBUS COMMIXTA
has pinnate leaves that are guaranteed to colour in the autumn, changing from green through orange and red to crimson.

left above and below
SORBUS AUCUPARIA
is one tough tree, growing on the sides of mountains with its roots clutching at the rocks and producing a crop of berries to feed every bird in the area.

Sorbus commixta

This tree is totally reliable for autumn colour, irrespective of the weather or fluctuations in temperature. In winter the 2.5cm (1in) long thin, pointed buds are shining red. The deciduous, 25cm (10in) long, pinnate leaves open copper-green, turning to deep glossy green. In early autumn the foliage becomes bright orange-red, then scarlet and finally deep crimson.

ascending branches result in a conical tree which, in later years, broadens considerably.

The variety 'Embley' is a smaller tree with deep red, autumn leaves that colour late, lasting on the tree until early winter. Large bunches of shiny, orange-red berries weigh down the branches.

Sorbus intermedia 'Brouwers'
SWEDISH WHITEBEAM

In truth, this tree has as much right to be named Norwegian whitebeam as Swedish: it is native to most of north-west Europe. The deciduous, 12.5cm (5in) long, glossy, dark green leaves are toothed, with small lobes close to the base and a grey tomentum on the underside. Clusters of white flowers appear in late spring followed by small, oblong, bright red berries.

This variety has an upright growth habit with ascending branches. Its parent, *S. intermedia*, forms a round-headed tree. It is totally hardy, tolerating coastal sites, cold, exposed hillsides or the air pollution of the city. Most soils, with the exception of waterlogged and alkaline ground, are

The colour change starts along the edge of the leaves, working towards the centre to give each leaf a multi-coloured effect. In late spring the small, white flowers appear in clusters 15cm (6in) across followed in autumn by large, erect bunches of small, spherical, orange-red berries.

S. commixta will grow in most soils with the exception of waterlogged ground. It prefers a rich, acid soil in an open, sunny site. It will grow to a height of 10m (33ft) with a mature spread of 6m (20ft). Its

SORBUS SARGENTIANA
is another species that is generous with its berries, providing you with a brilliant display if the birds don't get there first. The picture on page 45 shows this wonderful tree in all its autumn glory.

suitable. In a deep, fertile, well-drained soil it will thrive, growing to a height of 8m (26ft) with a spread of 5m (16ft).

Sorbus sargentiana

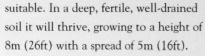

This mountain-ash-type sorbus is my favourite and that is saying a lot, because I am in love with all of the genus. It was found in China by plant hunter E. H. Wilson and is a generous tree, displaying its wares for 12 months of the year. The deciduous, 35cm (14in) long, dark green, pinnate leaves turn orange-red and finally crimson in autumn. White flowers in early summer are followed by large clusters of bright red autumn berries which may last, if the birds leave them, until early winter.

The large winter buds are sticky like the buds of horse chestnut but a deep red colour, opening in early spring to reveal young, red-tinted foliage.

It will grow in most soil types with the exception of alkaline and waterlogged ground but prefers a deep, well-drained, fertile site in a sunny situation, reaching 10m (33ft) in height with the same spread.

above and right
SORBUS VILMORINII
Is ideal for the small garden and guaranteed to fruit every year.

Sorbus vilmorinii

This is the most manageable sorbus I know. I would, with no disrespect intended, call it a ladies' tree. Dainty and pretty, it will grace any garden and, unlike some ladies, it has no bad habits.

The delicate, 15cm (6in) long, fern-like deciduous, pinnate leaves are dark, glossy green. They often grow in clusters spaced along the stems. In early autumn they turn red and purple, often lasting into early winter. The 10cm (4in) wide clusters of white flowers appear in early summer and are followed by drooping clusters of fruit in autumn. The fruit ripens from rose-red through clear pink before turning to white flushed with red.

It will succeed in most soils but prefers a deep, fertile, acid soil with good drainage. While it is happy in full sun it looks best in light shade. This is a good sorbus for the small garden, growing to a height of 5m (16ft) with the same spread.

Stewartii pseudocamellia

FALSE CAMELLIA

Sometimes labelled Stuartii, this tree was named for the eighteenth-century Earl of Bute, John Stuart. It is a great tree for a mixed planting and deserves to be better known and more frequently used in gardens. The mature, flaking bark reveals an attractive winter patchwork of pale red, brown and grey. In autumn, the deciduous 10cm (4in) long, finely toothed, dark green leaves turn to golden yellow, orange, red and finally purple before falling. Cup-shaped, 5cm (2in), single, white flowers appear in the leaf axils at the height of summer. Their creamy-white anthers give the flowers the appearance of a wild rose. Each flower lasts only a few days but the succession of blooms may be spread over six to eight weeks.

It is a fast-growing tree that dislikes being transplanted. Buy it as a small container-grown plant and try to avoid disturbing the roots when planting. Plant it in a moist, free-draining, acid soil with lots of added humus such as leaf mould or compost. It prefers its roots to be cool and shaded, making it an ideal tree for the front of a woodland planting. Protect it from cold winds, especially in spring. At maturity, the tree has an open habit, growing to 18m (60ft) with a spread of 7m (23ft).

Styrax japonicus

JAPANESE SNOWBELL

A tree made for gardens. Although widely planted in Korea, Japan and America it is, unfortunately, little used in Britain. It was once prized for its fragrant sap, which was used for incense. The deciduous, 10cm (4in) long, glossy, dark green leaves turn yellow, orange or red in late autumn. The leaves on flowering stems are smaller. In early to mid-summer the creamy-white, bell-shaped, fragrant flowers hang in clusters along the underside of one-year-old branches. Occasionally the flowers may be tinged with pale pink. Pairs of leaves perch vertically, like green butterflies on the upper side of the branch above the flower cluster. The flowers are followed in late summer by small pale green, oblong fruit. They hang on long stalks each containing one or two seeds. Whenever possible plant this tree on a height or a bank. Viewed from below the flower show in summer is magic.

The snowbell tree is totally hardy and can tolerate most soil conditions providing there is no lime present. It prefers a deep, fertile, free-draining soil with lots of humus added. Plant it in full sun, sheltered from cold winds. It matures to form an open-headed tree with the branches almost growing horizontally. The height may be 8m (26ft) with almost the same spread of up to 7m (23ft).

Syringa pekinensis

LILAC

I couldn't leave out one of my favourite trees for fragrance, the lilac.

The deciduous, 9cm (3in) long, dark green leaves have no great attributes and are hardly missed in winter. This species has creamy-white, fragrant flowers carried in dense, crowded panicles 20cm (8in) long, in early summer. They form mainly at the tips of the arching stems weighing the branches down. Dead flowers should be removed to tidy up the plant and encourage next year's blooms.

left
STYRAX JAPONICUS
Even when the older branches become horizontal this is a compact tree, which will fit into most gardens.

It enjoys a moist, alkaline, well-drained, fertile soil. Plant it in a position in full sun and close to a path where its perfume will be appreciated but far enough back not to need regular pruning. It will quickly grow to a height and spread of 5m (16ft), making it ideal for a small garden where space is limited. 'Pendula' is a smaller weeping form with pendulous branches.

Tamarix ramosissima 'Pink Cascade'

TAMARISK

This deciduous shrub or small tree forms a graceful plant. The tiny, pointed, feathery foliage appears in late spring on thin, arching, red-brown stems. In late summer and autumn the small pink flowers are carried in large plumes. This plant is tougher than it looks, making it ideal for planting in exposed sites and close to the sea. It needs a light, sandy, well-drained soil in full sun and dislikes cold, draughty sites. Prune hard after planting. It will reach a height and spread of 5m (16ft).

Tetradium daniellii

CHINESE EUODIA

Sometimes labelled as *Euodia daniellii*, this tree is virtually unknown in British gardens. It has a lot to offer and, where space permits, it should be considered as a specimen tree. The dull, dark grey bark is smooth throughout the life of the tree. It is different to most trees in that there are no bud scales. Instead the leaves are tightly folded and covered in a protective mat of purple-brown hairs throughout the winter. The deciduous, 40cm (16in) long, pinnate leaves are glossy, dark green turning to a butter yellow in autumn. The leaf stalk is mauve-pink. It is one of the few, and among the best, of the late-summer and early-autumn flowering trees. Small, pungent, white flowers with yellow anthers are carried in flat heads up to 15cm (6in) across. They are followed in late autumn by clusters of small russet-red berries that turn to black, remaining on the tree for most of the winter.

It will grow quickly in most soils, with the exception of waterlogged ground. It prefers a moist, deep, well-drained, fertile soil. Totally hardy, it flowers and fruits best following a long hot summer. Plant it in a sheltered situation in full sun where it will grow to a height and spread of 13m (43ft).

Tilia petiolaris
WEEPING SILVER LIME

Also listed by nurserymen as *Tilia tomentosa* 'Petiolaris', this is my favourite lime. As a young tree its weeping branch habit and pendulous shoots have an air of containment, but be warned, this is not a tree for small gardens or the faint-hearted. It will quickly outgrow most other trees.

The deciduous, 7.5cm (3in) long, dark, green leaves are hairy white on the underside and held on long stalks. On a clear, breezy day, with a blue sky, it makes a remarkable sight, with the white and green of the shivering leaves reflecting the sun. Aphids (greenfly) love all of the limes with the exception of *Tilia* x *euchlora* and, as with *T. platyphyllos* 'Rubra', they make a mess of the leaves, blackening them with honeydew and soiling everything directly below the tree. Small, pendant, sweetly fragrant, pale yellow flowers are held in clusters of up to 10 in late summer. Unfortunately the flowers are narcotic to bumble bees and more often than not cause their death.

Weeping silver lime prefers an alkaline soil but will tolerate being planted in acid ground. Avoid soils that dry out in summer. Plant it in sun or light shade with protection from cold winds. Its ultimate height is 30m (100ft) with a spread of 18m (60ft).

Tilia platyphyllos 'Rubra'
RED-TWIGGED LIME

This tree's parent, *T. platyphyllos*, is known as the broad-leaved lime and since its leaves are the same size, 'Rubra' should really be named the broad-leaved, red-twigged lime.

The stately homes and castles of England would not be the same without avenues of limes. The French love their *tilleuls*, the Americans call them basswoods and the Germans have introduced the world to their lindens.

The young shoots are a bright red, ageing to brownish-red. They are particularly effective when viewed in winter without leaf. In a substantial, deciduous hedge they are impressive throughout the winter. Clip a hedge to shape it in spring, to allow the new shoots all summer to grow. The deciduous, 7.5-15cm (3-6in) ovate, dark green leaves are pale green and hairy on the underside. In autumn they turn a soft yellow. Small, sweetly scented, pale yellow flowers hang in clusters in early to mid-summer followed by small fruit.

This tree can tolerate pollution but care is needed when choosing a suitable city planting site. It is prone to aphid attack, resulting in exuded honeydew that marks the paintwork of cars parked close by. It is tolerant of most soil conditions with the exception of very dry ground and enjoys

an alkaline soil. A well-fertilized soil will encourage growth, resulting in extended red shoots. Grow it in full sun or partial shade in a site sheltered from cold winds, where it will grow to a height of 25m (80ft) with a spread of 17m (55ft).

Ulmus x hollandica 'Dampieri Aurea'

GOLDEN DUTCH ELM

In Holland this elm is known as *U. x hollandica* 'Wredei'. I can also tell you that the W is pronounced as a V. Apart from that gem of information, this species of elm is confusing and has many forms that differ sufficiently to be noticeable. Elms from Holland, Belgium, France and Germany are all classified as *Ulmus x hollandica*.

The deciduous, double-toothed, 7-10cm (3-4in) long, bright yellow leaves of the golden Dutch elm hold their colour through the summer, turning to an insipid green-gold in autumn. The leaves are densely crowded in short laterals. Strong sunlight will scorch the leaves and turn them brown, so plant it in light shade, in moist, well-drained, fertile soil with protection from cold winds.

It forms a many-branched, narrow conical tree ideal for planting in gardens where space is limited and will grow to 9m (30ft) with a spread of 2m (6ft 6in).

TILIA PETIOLARIS
Fragrant, pale yellow flowers appear in summer followed by attractive seed pods.

CONIFERS

This book is like my garden: there is not enough room for all the plants. Unfortunately the space reserved for conifers is limited. As in the garden, I dislike crowding the plants and I have been selective with my varieties, giving each one the space it needs. I am aware I have left out some favourites but, as they are well known, you don't need this book to tell you about them.

CEDRUS LIBANI 'SARGENTII'
Very effective when used as ground cover over large rocks. It moulds itself, leaving an air of mystery as to what it is covering.

Abies koreana
KOREAN FIR

If you are impatient then this is the conifer for you. It has the decency to produce its beautiful cones from an early age. Plants only 1m (3ft) high often start to bear cones. By the time they have grown to eye level the cones weigh the branches down. Small, shiny, dark green leaves cover the upper side of the stem, curving upwards. The underside of the leaf is marked with two broad silver-white lines. The male flowers are dark red and insignificant. The female flowers may be deep purple or pink, followed by candle-like, cylindrical, deep blue or purple upright cones 5-7.5cm (2-3in) long, which turn brown before falling. They exude beads of clear resin that shine like frozen raindrops in sunlight.

Fir (*Abies*) and spruce (*Picea*) can be difficult to distinguish. A simple, foolproof method is to look at the cones. Those of the fir are always above the branch while those on a spruce hang down below.

This fir enjoys a spell of cold weather, looking spectacular with a coating of frost or snow. It prefers an alkaline, moist, deep, well-drained, fertile soil in a sunny site. Slow-growing, it forms a pyramid shape, reaching a height of 10m (33ft) with a spread of 6m (20ft).

Cedrus atlantica 'Glauca Pendula'
WEEPING BLUE ATLAS CEDAR

This cedar takes its name from the mountain range in North Africa. There, the species *Cedrus atlantica* grows to be an enormous tree of 40m (133ft) in height. The blue form, 'Glauca', reaches a similar size when mature but with silver-blue foliage. Neither of these giants is suitable for a small or even a medium-sized garden.

The weeping form is much more compact and quite at home in all but the smallest of gardens. It is a beautiful conifer with many uses in the garden. Left to its own devices it will make a very effective evergreen ground carpeting. It will be happy following the contours of a rockery, draping itself over rocks or tumbling down the face of a wall. Trained upright on a stake or stout bamboo as a single-stemmed tree, it may be allowed to weep when it reaches a desirable height of up to 3m (10ft).

The 2.5cm (1in) long, sharply pointed, narrow leaves are a deep silver-blue and held in tight whorls of 30-40 all along the stem. The young branches are pendulous. If they are to be trained to form an arch, they need to be held in position on a frame until the stems become rigid. The main leader is as anxious to reach the ground as its side shoots and will grow at least 30cm (12in) a year. If shaping is required, do the work in late spring.

This stunning conifer will tolerate dry soil and enjoys a position in full sun. It will usually weep from a height of 3m (10ft). The ultimate spread depends on how it is trained but 4m (13ft) is easily attained.

Cedrus deodara 'Golden Horizon'
GOLDEN DEODAR CEDAR

The deodar originates in the Himalayas where it makes an enormous tree. It is not a tree for any but the largest of gardens. 'Golden Horizon' is a Dutch selection and is a small grafted plant. This leads to a variation in the growth habit of young plants. When grown in a sunny site the 5cm (2in) long leaves are bright sulphur-

yellow in summer, fading to green-yellow in winter. When planted in shade the plant loses most of its yellow tone and the leaves stay a pale blue-green.

This conifer dislikes waterlogged soil. It prefers a well-drained or dry soil and grows well in impoverished, gravelly ground. As a young plant it is prostrate, eventually becoming semi-prostrate and growing to a height of 2m (6ft 6in) with a spread of 7m (23ft).

Unfortunately it has a habit of throwing out strong upright branches. If these are not removed they will grow away, overpowering the weaker growth and forming a large tree.

Cedrus libani 'Sargentii'

The species *Cedrus libani* is the cedar of Lebanon and trees estimated to be at least 2,000 years old grow on the slopes of Mount Lebanon. They have been grown in Britain since the mid-seventeenth century and were used by Capability Brown. 'Sargentii' is a rather less noticeable variety, growing slowly to form a dwarf mounded conifer. For the first few years after planting it remains prostrate, with sharp, blue-green leaves 2.5cm (1in) long. It is ideal for planting in the rock garden and makes an attractive display tumbling over a wall to a lower level.

It prefers a well-drained soil in a sunny situation. It cannot tolerate waterlogged ground. When young, the new spring growths are liable to damage from cold wind. Its maximum height is 80cm (32in) with an impressive spread of 4m (13ft). The variety 'Pendula' makes a taller-growing conifer with trailing branches.

Chamaecyparis lawsoniana 'Columnaris'

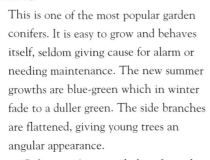

This is one of the most popular garden conifers. It is easy to grow and behaves itself, seldom giving cause for alarm or needing maintenance. The new summer growths are blue-green which in winter fade to a duller green. The side branches are flattened, giving young trees an angular appearance.

'Columnaris' is a good plant for making a statement or providing height in small gardens and heather beds. It may also be planted at 45cm (18in) spacings to form a dense, easily maintained, compact, evergreen hedge. A well-drained soil with added nutrients suits it best, where it will grow to 10m (33ft) with a spread of 1m (3ft). The variety 'Pelt's Blue' forms an even tighter, columnar plant with a spread of 75cm (30in) and deep blue leaves.

Chamaecyparis lawsoniana 'Ellwoodii'

This popular conifer has grey-green foliage turning blue-green in winter. It is named after the head gardener who discovered the juvenile form growing on C. *lawsoniana* and propagated from it. Although it is not actually a dwarf conifer it is frequently mistreated by being planted in small containers and rockeries.

As a young conifer it is slow-growing forming a compact plant with several leaders. At maturity the shape may vary considerably from plant to plant, depending where the cuttings were taken from the parent tree. Often conical in shape, it may be squat or columnar and may vary in height up to 8m (26ft) with a spread of 2m (6ft 6in).

It will be short-lived if planted in water-logged ground, preferring moist, free-draining, fertile soil in sun or partial shade. It may be grown in a large container for a number of years but eventually it will need to be planted out in the garden.

Chamaecyparis lawsoniana 'Kilmacurragh'

This variety was raised at Kilmacurragh, County Wicklow in Ireland. It forms a magnificent tree resembling an Italian cypress (*Cupressus sempervirens*). The young foliage is bright green, turning to dark green with age. Short ascending branches give the tree strength with resistance to heavy snow falls. It is totally hardy and ideal as a first line of defence for windswept gardens. It prefers a moist, well-drained, acid soil in sun or partial shade. Fast-growing, it will reach 12m (40ft) in height with a spread of 5m (16ft).

Chamaecyparis lawsoniana 'Lutea'

You know where you are with this conifer. It has been grown in Britain since the nineteenth century and is perfectly behaved, forming a wide columnar tree

above
CHAMAECYPARIS LAWSONIA 'COLUMNARIS'
Imagine a long, sweeping avenue, lined on either side with well-spaced 'Columnaris'. No maintenance and getting better every year.

right
CHAMAECYPARIS LAWSONIA 'LUTEA'
One of the best golden 'lawsons'. Don't cut into the old wood as it won't produce new side shoots.

with a narrow, open top. The golden yellow foliage keeps its colour all year and is formed in flattened sprays.

Plant it in a well-drained, fertile soil in full sun. It dislikes waterlogged or alkaline soil. It will grow to 15m (50ft) in height with a spread of 4m (13ft). Grown as a hedge it makes a wonderful dense, wind-resistant screen.

The dwarf variety 'Lutea Nana' grows slowly to 2m (6ft 6in), forming a golden-yellow, conical plant.

Chamaecyparis lawsoniana 'Minima Aurea'

Rogers Nursery in Hampshire, England introduced several seedling conifers in the first half of the twentieth century and this gem was one of them. It grows slowly to form a conical shape with short, rigid branches and firm golden-yellow foliage. When mature it forms a round-topped dome. Providing the soil is acid, fertile and not waterlogged, this conifer will keep its shape and colour for a lifetime. It should be planted in full sun to encourage the foliage to remain yellow all year. Its maximum height is about 2m (6ft 6in) with a spread of 1m (3ft). 'Aurea Densa' is another seedling from the same nursery and is very similar in colour, size and shape.

Chamaecyparis lawsoniana 'Pembury Blue'

If not the best, then this is one of the best of the larger blue Lawson cypresses. It forms a conical tree with arching branches of silvery blue and new growths are bright blue. Growing at 30cm (12in) a year, 'Pembury Blue' makes a fine specimen on the lawn or as a backdrop mixed with golden foliage cypresses such as 'Stewartii'.

above
CHAMAECYPARIS OBTUSA 'NANA'
This gem can spend its life in a large container, repotting every few years in a soil-based compost.

It prefers a deep, well-drained, moist, fertile soil. The blue colour is best if the tree is planted in full sun but it tolerates light shade. It will grow to a height of 15m (50ft) with a spread of 3m (10ft).

Chamaecyparis obtusa 'Nana'
DWARF HINOKI CYPRESS

Chamaecyparis obtusa, the parent of this dwarf conifer, is considered sacred by those who follow the Japanese Shinto faith. I have enormous respect for 'Nana'. It is one of the very best of the truly miniature chamaecyparis for planting in the rock garden, scree bed or shallow container. It may also be used with great success for bonsai growing.

Slow-growing, it eventually forms a flat-topped plant. The deep, dark green foliage appears as tiers of sprays of cup-shaped fans.

If planting a dry rockery site, add extra moisture-retentive compost to prevent the roots suffering from drought. It dislikes cold spring winds and even moderate falls of snow will destroy the shape. Brush off snow before it accumulates or freezes on the foliage.

The tree will eventually grow to 60cm (24in) in height with a spread of 1m (3ft). There is a similar but fast-growing variety named 'Nana Gracilis', which is often sold as 'Nana', but will reach a height of 3m (10ft). 'Nana Aurea' has sulphur-yellow foliage and grows to 2m (6ft 6in) in height.

Chamaecyparis pisifera 'Boulevard'

Bred in a nursery in Newport, America in the twentieth century, 'Boulevard' was the first conifer I grew. Better still, I propagated it from a cutting. This only confirms that it is one of the easiest conifers to grow. I still love it and would argue that, when grown properly, it is one of the best 'all-round' garden conifers.

'Boulevard' is a sport of C.*p*. 'Squarrosa' with juvenile foliage. When young it is pyramidal, later growing to form a dense conical plant. The silvery-blue foliage is as soft as new wool. In winter it turns to grey-green with a purple tinge. It responds to pruning on an annual basis to maintain its shape, which otherwise becomes straggly. Feeding with a high nitrogen feed in late spring increases the blue colour.

When necessary it may be successfully grown for a few years in a container, providing the compost is not allowed to dry out. It prefers a moist, well-fed, acid or neutral soil in a sheltered situation in full sun and grows to 8m (26ft) with a spread of 3m (10ft).

Chamaecyparis pisifera 'Filifera Aurea'

GOLDEN THREAD-LEAF CYPRESS

Not to be confused with 'Filifera Aurea Nana' which is quite dwarf, this conifer is of medium height and ideal for average-sized gardens. During the first few years growth may be slow, creating the wrong impression. Once it settles down, it quickly forms a substantial pyramid with thin, bright yellow, pendulous foliage that deepens to golden yellow in winter. If planted in a position in full sun the foliage may scorch. Sited in front of dark green evergreens such as other conifers or holly trees it will, during winter, stand out like a bright light.

Early pruning to remove awkward branches allows the plant to be shaped. More mature trees may be pruned in late spring, after all risk of frost is over, to keep them to a suitable size. Cuttings taken

from side branches sometimes form small globular plants which some nurseries used to sell as 'Aurea Nana'. Later they grow to normal size, causing more confusion.

It prefers a moist, fertile, well-drained, acid soil in partial shade. Unpruned, it will grow to 8m (26ft) in height with a spread of 6m (20ft).

Chamaecyparis thyoides 'Ericoides'

WHITE FALSE CYPRESS

This is a beautiful dwarf variety of C. *thyoides* with a compact habit of growth. It is slow-growing, eventually forming a conical shape. The branches are

upright and stiff with soft, sea-green juvenile foliage. In winter it blushes to a deep plum-purple.

It is not a very hardy plant succeeding best in a sheltered position. The shape will be damaged by snow left to lie and it can not tolerate frost or cold spring winds. Choose a site sheltered from the morning sun and a wet but not a waterlogged soil. Shallow, alkaline ground is not to 'Ericoides' liking.

At maturity it may reach 2m (6ft 6in) in height with a spread of 1m (3ft). Other dwarf varieties with a rounded habit and good winter colour include 'Rubicon' and 'Heatherbun'.

Cryptomeria japonica 'Elegans'
JAPANESE CEDAR

Mr Thomas Lobb, plant-hunter and brother of the more famous William, discovered a number of plants in Japan and Borneo. He sent this conifer to the Veitch nurseries in England in 1854 and it has been popular in gardens ever since. Young plants have an attractive shape with the main branches ascending. Later they tend to sprawl, with the branches spreading out and then up. Juvenile foliage is a fresh, pale green and soft to the touch. In winter it turns to a deep plum-purple, the inner foliage remaining dark green. The fibrous bark is a bright orange-cinnamon and peels in thin shreds.

Plant this conifer in deep, fertile, moist soil, making sure that it doesn't dry out. It is not fully hardy and should be given some shelter from biting cold winds. A sunny site will ensure good winter colour, while pruning to curtail the more vigorous branches will improve its shape.

Designed into the garden with green

left
CHAMAECYPARIS THYOIDES 'ERICOIDES'
If there were seven dwarf cypresses this one would be 'Bashful'. In late autumn it's foliage blushes to plum-purple.

below
CRYPTOMERIA JAPONICA 'ELEGANS'
The foliage looks spikey but is soft to the touch. Leave space for the branches to dip-down to the ground.

and golden conifers as a backdrop, it makes a spectacular display in winter with the weak, low sun as a spotlight. It will grow to a height of 8m (26ft) with a spread of 5m (16ft).

The variety C. j. 'Lobbii', a beautiful medium-sized, pyramidal conifer, has glossy, dark green foliage that remains green in winter. The branches are well spaced with erect clumps of foliage at their tips. The cones, up to 2.5cm (1in) across, occasionally sprout while still on the tree, producing strange growths up to 5cm (2in) long.

Cunninghamia lanceolata
CHINA FIR

Named for plant hunter James Cunningham, who saw and described the tree during an expedition to China in the eighteenth century, this is an uncommon conifer in Britain and elsewhere. It deserves to be better known and more frequently

planted in larger gardens. It is quick-growing with a straight trunk and is one of China's main timber-producing trees. The bark is brown, flaking off mature trees to expose the reddish inner bark.

The evergreen 7.5cm (3in) long, leathery, glossy bright green leaves are sharply pointed with two white lines of stomata on the underside. The leaves sprout out of the stems at all angles. As they die, they turn brown and stay on the branch so the foliage appears green-brown. The rigid branches are horizontal, giving the tree an open look.

Mature trees may develop multiple leaders and these need to be reduced to one, to avoid spoiling the shape. Lower branches often die and fall off, giving the tree a raised head.

The China fir prefers a deep, moist, well-drained, fertile soil. Cold winds and frost may brown the leaves and kill the young tips of branches but new shoots will form and grow away. Plant in a sheltered site in full sun in areas of high rainfall. It will grow to a height of 20m (66ft) with a spread of 6m (20ft).

x Cuprocyparis leylandii 'Robinson's Gold'

GOLDEN LEYLAND CYPRESS

Discovered and named after the head gardener of Belvoir Forest Park, Belfast in 1975, this is still the best of the golden leylands and is a brother to the famous – or infamous – green x *Cuprocyparis leylandii*, which is a cross between *Cupressus macrocarpa* and *Xanthocyparis nootkatensis*. Green leylandii gets a bad press because it quickly grows to be an enormous tree. The truth is that, in the right situation, it is a marvellous plant.

X CUPROCYPARIS LEYLANDII 'ROBINSON'S GOLD'
If you want a fast growing golden conifer this is the best. But a word of warning; it must be clipped frequently to prevent it becoming a large tree.

The problem lies with the nurseries and garden centres that sell the trees without pointing out their ultimate size, as well as their speedy growth. People also plant them in totally inappropriate sites.

'Robinson's Gold' has foliage of bright golden yellow, turning a deeper yellow in winter. It will grow well in any soil except those which are waterlogged and is totally hardy. Close to the coast, foliage facing the sea will be scorched by salt-laden winds. Given good soil conditions it will grow at least 60cm (2ft) a year to a height of 25m (80ft) and spread to 6m (20ft).

There are many varieties of the green leylandii, most of them growing to over 30m (100ft). They are ideal for planting for a quick screen or evergreen hedge but need regular clipping to keep them within bounds. Dark blue-green or dull grey-green foliage is carried in slightly drooping sprays and is variable depending from which stock the cuttings have been taken. 'Haggerston Grey' has grey-green leaves while 'Leighton Green' foliage is bright green. The fast-growing variety 'Rostrevor' originated in the village of that name in County Down, Northern Ireland in 1870. It has bright green foliage and was probably the first of the leylandii.

Cupressus macrocarpa 'Goldcrest'
GOLDEN MONTEREY CYPRESS

Unlike the chamaecyparis, this is a true cypress. *C.macrocarpa* has travelled well from its native California and is a better plant for the move. It is fast growing, making a large, open, tough plant around the coasts of Britain. In Ireland it forms a more branched tree without losing any of the height.

'Goldcrest' forms a compact, narrow, columnar tree with golden yellow, feathery, juvenile foliage. In winter the gold turns to pale yellow.

Plant it in a moist, well-drained, fertile soil in a position in full sun. To prevent browning of the foliage it should be sheltered from cold winds. It makes a superb dot or specimen conifer for seaside gardens, growing to 5m (16ft) with a spread of 2.5m (8ft). This variety has better colour and shape than two similar varieties, 'Donard Gold' and 'Lutea'.

There is another true cypress well worth growing: the Tecate cypress (*Cupressus guadalupensis*) from the Guadeloupe Islands and southern California. It is a stunning, fast-growing evergreen conifer

with peeling, red-pink bark that flakes off in small pieces. The fragrant, blue-green foliage is sharply pointed. Avoid planting it in waterlogged ground. It is not fully hardy and needs a sheltered site in full sun. It will grow to 12m (40ft) with a spread of 4m (13ft).

Ginkgo biloba 'Princeton Sentry'
MAIDENHAIR TREE

I must admit to being sexist. The only reason I have listed the variety 'Princeton Sentry' is because it is male. The fact that it differs only from the species in shape, being narrow and upright, is of no importance. What is important is that the male variety doesn't produce fruit and if you have ever had to breathe in the odour of ripe ginkgo fruit you will also prefer a male tree.

Apart from that, the deciduous ginkgo has a lot going for it. It is older than the hills – it saw them formed. It has been around for longer than most living things. The distinctive leaf is fossilised in rock in Scarborough, Yorkshire, and the tree is known to have been growing happily 160 million years ago. The first British ginkgo since prehistoric times was planted in 1760 in Kew Gardens and is still there today.

The grey-barked trunk is usually straight when young, branching later to form a spreading tree. The pale green, fan-shaped leaves are up to 12.5cm (5in) across with fan-shaped veins. The leaves hang down on long stalks with a notch in the middle of the leaf that almost splits young leaves in two.

In autumn the leaves slowly turn to a soft butter-yellow. The green gradually disappears, providing a variegated

CUPRESSUS MACROCARPA 'GOLDCREST' needs a good root run. Where the roots are confined it may blow out of the ground.

appearance. There isn't a hint of brown or other autumn shade and the display is short-lived but worth seeing. Male plants produce clusters of 7.5cm (3in) long yellow catkins at the same time as the leaves. Female trees produce small pale green flowers as the leaves emerge. Ginkgo fruit are 2.5cm (1in) long, green-yellow and plum-shaped. The nut within is edible but the ripe fruit has a most unpleasant smell.

The tree prefers a moist, deep, fertile, well-drained soil. It is very hardy, tolerating cold, windy sites but thrives in a site in full sun. 'Princeton Sentry' will grow to a height of 20m (66ft) with a spread of 5m (16ft).

Juniperus chinensis 'Spartan'
CHINESE JUNIPER

The Chinese juniper is the parent of many excellent varieties, one of the best being 'Spartan'. Found in the Monrovia nursery in California in 1961, it has both juvenile and adult foliage. It forms a dense, narrow, columnar tree with pungent, dark green foliage. The blue-bloomed fruit are attractive but appear only on older trees.

This conifer will tolerate the poorest of dry ground and will succeed in all soils except waterlogged ground. It prefers a site in full sun with low levels of rain. It will grow to a height of 10m (33ft) with a spread of 1.2m (4ft).

Juniperus communis 'Compressa'
NOAH'S ARK JUNIPER

This has to be the best-behaved conifer ever to have graced a rockery or alpine bed. It is compact, dwarf, dense, columnar and very slow-growing. The long, thin, mid-green leaves have a silver band in the upper surface and are dark green on the underside. If the foliage turns brown in summer,

inspect the tree for red spider mite.

It prefers a well-drained soil in full sun. Don't plant it in heavy, wet soil. It will suffer from dieback if planted in an exposed site subject to cold winds and frost.

It will slowly grow to a height of 80cm (32in) with a spread of 45cm (18in).

There is a larger more hardy variety 'Suecica Nana', with bright blue-green foliage that grows to a height of 85cm (34in) with a spread of 60cm (24 in).

Juniperus communis 'Hibernica'
IRISH JUNIPER

The Irish form of the common juniper has, like all other varieties, juvenile foliage. Its other claim to fame is that its berries are used in the making of gin. They are green in the first year, turning blue-black in the second year. Although J. communis grows wild in many parts of Britain, its berries are no longer harvested for gin. 'Hibernica' forms a narrow, dense, columnar tree with ascending branches. The sharply pointed, light green leaves have silver bands on the upper surface and are blue-green on the underside. In winter the green deepens. Providing it is not planted in waterlogged ground, this conifer will tolerate most soils and is happy growing among rocks in a well-drained rockery or scree bed.

Although it is totally hardy, a heavy fall of snow will knock it out of shape, opening up the centre and exposing brown and dead foliage. It will grow to a height of 5m (16ft) with a spread of 60cm (24in).

below

JUNIPERUS COMMUNIS 'COMPRESSA'
Garden centres know that you will fall in love and want to take one home with you!

Juniperus horizontalis

CREEPING JUNIPER

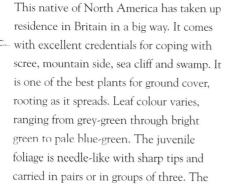

This native of North America has taken up residence in Britain in a big way. It comes with excellent credentials for coping with scree, mountain side, sea cliff and swamp. It is one of the best plants for ground cover, rooting as it spreads. Leaf colour varies, ranging from grey-green through bright green to pale blue-green. The juvenile foliage is needle-like with sharp tips and carried in pairs or in groups of three. The wild plant produces dark blue fruit.

This conifer can tolerate the worst of sites and is completely hardy to wind and frost but prefers a well-drained soil in full sun. It may be prostrate or procumbent, growing to a height of 30-75cm (12-30in) with a spread that is more or less indefinite.

There are many cultivated varieties: 'Bar Harbor' is prostrate with blue-green foliage; 'Blue Chip' is prostrate with silvery blue feathery foliage; 'Wiltonii' is one of the best ground-covering conifers, forming a carpet of blue.

Juniperus scopulorum 'Skyrocket'

Sometimes labelled *J. virginiana* 'Skyrocket', this conifer suits its name, which is so much more descriptive than 'Columnaris' or 'Fastigate'. It grows at a steady pace to form a tall, narrow, evergreen pillar. The scale-like, glaucous, grey-green leaves are pointed and lie flat along the stem.

It should be planted in a moist, well-drained soil in full sun. It dislikes areas with high rainfall, preferring a dry atmosphere. When grown in a fertile soil with plenty of moisture it forms a broader tree. Lying snow bends the branches, spoiling the shape of the tree. Where

above
JUNIPERUS SQUAMATA 'MEYERI'
Beautiful when young, this juniper ages with style.

below
JUNIPERUS SCOPULORUM 'SKYROCKET'
A well-behaved conifer that, like the rest of us, spreads a little with age.

heavy falls of snow are likely the tree should be tied-in every winter and the ties kept in place until spring.

It will grow to a height of 6m (20ft) with a spread of 60cm (24in).

Juniperus squamata 'Meyeri'

Found in a Chinese garden in 1914 by Frank Meyer, this tree is known locally as the fish-tail juniper. It has a distinctive shape with upright branches and young arching growths. The centre of the plant is open, revealing the old brown, dead leaves. This can make the tree look straggly if it is not pruned to shape.

At the base the foliage is silver-blue in summer, turning pale purple-blue in winter.

It is not a fussy plant, growing well in most soils, especially dry, gravelly soil. It is hardy but dislikes biting cold winds. It will grow to a height of 8m (26ft) with a spread of 3m (10ft).

Larix decidua

EUROPEAN LARCH, COMMON LARCH

Some trees are so plentiful as to be overlooked and this deciduous conifer is one of them. It is called common larch because there are whole forests of them in some parts of Britain and millions in Scotland.

In spring the emerging soft, pale green whorls of leaves embarrass other brasher trees. To see those same hectares in autumn when the golden-brown foliage catches the low, weak, late autumn sun is unforgettable. If another reason is needed for larch's inclusion in this book, let it be

LARIX KAEMPFERI
It is easy to forgive this tree for not beeing evergreen. In early spring the blue-green foliage and elegant cones gladden the heart, while in autumn the soft deep yellow leaves carpet the ground before disappearing without leaving a mess.

its usefulness as a tough windbreak that filters every wind.

On older trees the smooth, grey bark becomes rough and scaly and the branches droop. Young growths are yellow with 4cm (1.5in) long leaves that are pale green when young.

Male and female flowers grow separately on the same tree, appearing before or at the same time as the leaves. The female cones are 4cm (1.5in) long, toffee-brown and ripen in the first year. After they shed their seed they remain on the tree for many years.

Common larch prefers a deep, moist, well-drained acid or neutral soil in full sun. If the soil is light or gravelly it will respond well to an application of high nitrogen fertiliser in late spring. It dislikes transplanting and is best planted as a one-year-old seedling. It prefers areas of high rainfall, growing to a height of 30m (100ft) with a spread of 20m (66ft).

Larix kaempferi

JAPANESE LARCH

The Japanese larch differs from the common one in having a more sturdy trunk and a dense crown of branches. The bark of young trees is almost red, turning to brown on older trees. In the second year the winter shoots are purple-red with a waxy bloom and when spotlighted by the winter sun, the tree appears to be purple.

In early spring the 4cm (1.5in) long, deciduous leaves appear blue-green on the upper surface with two white bands on the underside. In autumn the leaves turn orange-yellow before falling. The female flowers are red and cream followed by conical, rust brown, rosette-like cones with reflexed scales.

This larch dislikes a dry, alkaline soil, preferring a moist, well-drained fertile one. It is hardy and can tolerate cold winds and frost. It will grow to a height of 30m (100ft) with a spread of 6m (20ft).

Metasequoia glyptostroboides

DAWN REDWOOD

The discovery of this deciduous conifer is fascinating, romantic and incredible. It had been well known as a fossil of a leaf of a tree that grew 200 million years ago. In 1941 a living tree was found in central China but no one recognized it as the fossil tree until 1944. Seed was distributed in Britain in 1948 and there are now trees throughout the country.

The shaggy, cinnamon-brown bark is attractive and apparent even on young trees. The soft, bright green leaves appear in early spring and last well into autumn, turning deep pink and yellow-brown.

The dawn redwood will grow in most soils providing they do not dry out at any time. It prefers a warm climate, its rate of

METASEQUOIA GLYPTOSTROBOIDES
The soft green foliage scarcely covers the dead straight, central trunks coated in peeling red-brown bark.

growth slowing down in areas with cool summers. Plant it in a sunny position with shelter from cold winds. Its ultimate height can only be guessed at but the Chinese trees are claimed to be mature and are over 30m (100ft) at present with a spread of 7m (23ft). The variety 'National' forms a narrow conical tree with a predicted spread of 4m (13ft).

Picea abies 'Clanbrassiliana'

When you remember that *Picea abies* is the common spruce or Norway spruce, better known as the familiar Christmas tree, it is hard to believe that the miniature 'Clanbrassiliana' is remotely related. It was discovered on the Moira estate, near Lurgan, County Armagh in Northern Ireland in 1790 and moved by Lord Clanbrassil to his estate in Tullymore, on the side of Slieve Donard mountain in County Down. The original tree is still growing there.

It forms a slow-growing, dense conifer with a flattened top. The attractive winter buds are red-brown set off by dull, mid-green foliage. The overall shape is untidy with some shoots growing more quickly than others.

It prefers a moist, free-draining soil that is neutral or acid. Although it is a hardy conifer, a heavy fall of snow will leave the plant misshapen. It will grow to a height of 2m (6ft 6in) with a spread of 3m (10ft).

The variety 'Inversa' is commonly known as the drooping Norway spruce. It forms an amazing pendulous tree with the branches held tightly to the trunk and spilling over the ground when they can go no lower. The leaves are dark, dull green. It will grow to a height of 10m (33ft) with a spread of 1m (3ft).

Picea breweriana

BREWER'S WEEPING SPRUCE

Named for Professor Brewer of Yale University who discovered it in 1863, this unusual spruce is a spectacular sight when mature. Where space permits, it is ideal grown as a specimen on the lawn.

The branches are curved with thin trailing side shoots. The 2.5cm (1in) long, flat leaves are shining dark green on the upper surface with white stripes on the underside. The 10cm (4in) long, cylindrical cones are green, then purple, finally turning red-brown and hanging down in pairs.

It prefers a moist, well-drained, fertile soil in a sunny situation. Plant it as a young tree as it dislikes being transplanted later on. It will grow to 15m (50ft) with a spread of 4m (13ft).

left
PICEA BREWERIANA
Like the slender side branches the cones hang down, giving the tree a cowed look.

above
PICEA OMORIKA
If you can tolerate the height, this giant will fit into a small garden – the branches seemingly squeezing into the space.

Picea omorika

SERBIAN SPRUCE

I have fond memories of this tree, which comes from the mountains of what was Eastern Yugoslavia along the river Drina. I slept under a group of them without the benefit of a tent. Viewed lying flat on your back, or any other angle, it is a majestic conifer. Like a church steeple it climbs to a point, retaining its branches to the ground and hardly taking up 12 square metres of garden. If you can tolerate the height, then plant one and don't crowd it.

The short branches curve downwards and then change their minds and sweep upwards. The young shoots are fawny brown with broad, flat, shiny, blue-green needles that are white on the underside. The leaves have a peculiar arrangement, lying flat on the upper side of the shoot, while those on the underside hang down loosely. The 7.5cm (3in) long cones are blue-black when young, turning cinnamon-red as they age.

This conifer will grow in any type of soil and is perfectly happy in alkaline ground. It is totally hardy, growing in sun or shade.

If it is not congested by other plants it will hold its foliage to ground level. Although it makes a large tree, its slim shape reduces the shade area.

Fast-growing, it will quickly attain 15m (50ft) and go to a mature height of 25m (80ft) with a spread of 3m (10ft). Unfortunately it is prone to honey fungus disease (*Armillaria*) which can kill a mature tree in one season.

Picea pungens 'Koster'
KOSTER'S BLUE SPRUCE

This is one of the best of the blue spruces, although it starts life as a delinquent, unruly and disobedient, and seldom forms a leading shoot. The answer is to cane-up a side shoot. Once it learns to grow vertically it never looks back. Side shoots grow at different rates and in order to form a conical shape it is necessary to prune back those that are too long.

The shoots are orange or brown. New growths open from tight yellow-brown buds. The sharp, pointed new leaves are bright, glaucous blue-white. Older leaves are blue-green.

It prefers a moist, well-drained, deep, fertile soil in a sunny position. It is prone to attack by red spider mite, which browns and defoliates the centre of the plant.

This conifer has an open, loose habit with well-spaced branches, and grows to a height of 10m (33ft) with a spread of 5m (16ft). The variety 'Hoopsii' is slower-growing than 'Koster' with more startling blue foliage.

Picea sitchensis
SITKA SPRUCE

This is really a timber tree and not one that I would recommend for the average garden. It is in some ways the coastal version of the Norway spruce. As an evergreen conifer it has one great asset: it is as tough as they come. As a young tree up to 6m (20ft) high it makes a marvellous and not unattractive windbreak.

The stiff, sharply pointed leaves are bright green with two silvery bands on the underside. Cylindrical, 7.5-10cm (3-4 in) long, female cones are green, turning yellow-brown when mature.

It prefers an acid or neutral soil, growing well in wet ground. This conifer is best suited to climates with cool summers coupled with high rainfall figures. It is fast-growing to a height of 50m (166ft) with a spread of 12m (40ft).

Pinus mugo 'Pumilio'
DWARF MOUNTAIN PINE

A great dwarf mountain pine for planting in rockeries and scree beds. There seem to be two forms of this pine on the market. One is prostrate, hugging the ground; the other clone using the same

left

PICEA PUNGENS 'KOSTER'
may be subject to attacks of red spider mite, which defoliate the branches in the centre of the tree, spoiling the shape and colour. Even a healthy specimen needs a lot of discipline if it is to grow into an elegant tree.

name grows much higher, maturing at 3m (10ft).

Quite often 'Pumilio' refuses to form a leader. It is sometimes named the two-needle pine as the needles are held in pairs. Winter buds are long and conspicuous.

It is usually grown from seed, resulting in the leaves ranging from mid- to dark green and various shapes and sizes of plants. It prefers a well-drained site but will tolerate most conditions, including alkaline soil. It is totally hardy and is quite happy to be buried under snow for a few days. The height at maturity may range from 30cm (12in) to 2m (6ft 6in) with a spread of up to 3m (10ft).

Pinus ponderosa

WESTERN YELLOW PINE

The mature bark on this pine is outstanding. It is deeply fissured and may be pale pink or as dark as red-brown. The branches are long and spreading, with 25cm (10in) long, grey-green leaves held in groups of three in stiff bunches at the tips. The 15cm (6in) long dark brown cones hang in clusters.

It prefers a deep, well-drained soil in an open site in full sun. It can tolerate extremes of temperature and is unlikely to blow over during storms. Fast-growing for the first 15 years, it will reach a height of 35m (116ft) with a spread of 8m (26ft).

above
PINUS STROBUS
Old cones remain on the tree for up to 4–5 years, giving the impression of a bumper annual crop.

left
PINUS PONDEROSA
Deserves to be known as a fast-growing wind break. Its attractive bark lightens up any copse.

Pinus strobus

WEYMOUTH PINE

In Britain it is known as the Weymouth pine after Lord Weymouth, who introduced it to Longleat in Wiltshire. In America, however, it is labelled the eastern white pine. Its soft, white timber was in demand across Europe, resulting in whole forests disappearing to the axe and saw.

As a young pine it is conical, later turning more columnar. The grey-green, 7.5-12.5 cm (3-5in) long leaves are carried in groups of five. Cylindrical 7.5-15cm (3-6in) long, tapering, female cones are, at first, green, turning dark brown and curved. Each scale is edged in white resin, highlighting the cone. It matures in the second year and remains on the tree for years after shedding its seed.

This pine can not tolerate waterlogged or alkaline conditions, preferring a deep, well-drained soil in full sun. Eventually it will become too large for most garden sites but tolerates hard pruning and shaping. It will grow to a height of 30m (100ft) with a spread of 8m (26ft).

There are many varieties which are claimed to be dwarf. They start off with the best of intentions but soon speed up, forming large trees. 'Sea Urchin' is a true dwarf with long silver-blue leaves. 'Nana' will form a tree broader than it is tall with green leaves, silver-grey on the underside. It may grow to 5m (16ft) with a spread of 7m (23ft).

Pinus sylvestris

SCOTS PINE

This is the only pine native to Britain and almost exclusively to Scotland. It is also to be found across Europe as far as Turkey and Siberia and I'm sure they don't call it

Scots pine. Of all the pines in Europe this species was recognized as the best timber for a sailing ship's main mast.

As a young tree it is beautiful but as it grows, the trunk becomes bare with a mushroom head of branches. Old trees are frequently gnarled and twisted, creating a startling effect when seen against a night sky. The mature bark is scaly and comes in shades of cinnamon and dark brown. Bright blue-green needles 5-7.5cm (2-3in) long are held in slightly twisted pairs, becoming darker blue in summer. Female flowers are small and dark red. Male flowers are much more noticeable and a bright orange-red. Female cones are red, turning green and finally dark red-brown in the second year.

This conifer is tolerant of most soil conditions, including alkaline and acid, but dislikes waterlogged ground. It is totally hardy, making an excellent coastal windbreak. It dislikes hot, moist climates. It will grow to a height of 30m (100ft) with a spread of 9m (30ft). 'Aurea' is slower-growing with light green leaves turning bright yellow in winter. It will grow to 12m (40ft) with a spread of 4m (13ft).

Podocarpus salignus

WILLOW LEAF PODOCARP

Describing a podocarp isn't easy. It doesn't look like a conifer but, as its common name suggests, more like a willow. It is, however, evergreen so perhaps it is fair to say that its more like a yew tree but with paler leaves. Most conifers are monoecious, with both male and female flowers on the same plant, but this species is dioecious with male and female flowers on different plants.

It is a super conifer, native to Chile, with drooping branches and 5-10cm

above

PINUS SYLVESTRIS
Good looking when young and interesting when old, but it can look miserable in middle age as it loses its branches.

below

PODOCARPUS SALIGNUS
This unusual looking conifer is tolerant of most situations except for cold or waterlogged sites.

(2-4in) long, pale grey-green leaves. Sometimes it forms a bushy tree with no main trunk. If necessary it may be pruned hard so that new growths appear from the old trunk. The cones it produces are really waxy, purple-red fruits with a nut inside.

It can tolerate poor, deficient soil, alkaline or acid, but prefers a well-drained soil in a sheltered position in full sun. In cold, exposed gardens this tree will suffer. Under good conditions it will grow to 20m (66ft) with a spread of 8m (26ft).

Sequoia sempervirens 'Prostrata'

I like this plant because it is a 'kissing cousin' of the giant Californian redwood (*S. sempervirens*) which I would love but haven't got space for – it reaches a height of 30m (100ft) in Britain. This dwarf form originated as a sport in the University Botanic Gardens, Cambridge in England. It has bright glaucous green leaves, double ranked on red-brown shoots.

It prefers a moist, well-drained, fertile soil in a sunny position. It dislikes being transplanted so plant it as a small pot-grown conifer. The growth habit is flat, spreading on stiff branches. As it ages the branches build up in layers to form a plant 2m (6ft 6in) high, with a spread of 3m (10ft). 'Cantab' is a sport of 'Prostrata' with the same foliage and occurs when 'Prostrata' throws a strong growing shoot. It will grow to 14m (46ft).

Taxodium distichum

SWAMP CYPRESS

This deciduous conifer has a 'knees-up' at every opportunity. If it is planted beside tidal or fresh water it produces pneumatophores or specialized roots, which resemble knees sticking up out of the ground. It forms a conical tree with fawn-brown bark. The branches are brittle and most mature trees are misshapen through wind damage.

The 2.5cm (1in) long, pale green leaves are double ranked on the stems. They turn dark green in summer, then bright golden-brown in autumn before leaf fall. Green female cones turn black when ripe. The pendant male cones are red.

While this tree loves having its roots close to water it will grow perfectly well in a moist, fertile soil. The swamp cypress enjoys full sun or partial shade. When planted as a group and well spaced at 9m (30ft) the overall effect is rewarding. It is hardy although it does not do well in the north of Britain or Ireland. It will grow to a height of 30m (100ft) with a spread of 8m (26ft).

Taxus baccata

ENGLISH YEW

Take care when planting this tree. Almost all parts are poisonous to animals and humans. Birds eat the fruit without mishap because the seed passes through intact – the seed is poisonous but its fleshy surround isn't. I love yew but have to admit it can look a bit dour. It is a sombre-looking evergreen and has, in the past, been planted in many graveyards. There are specimen trees in Britain that are more than 1,000 years old and still growing.

The leaves are dark green on the upper side, pale green on the underside. The fleshy, bright red fruit or aril contains a single, green seed and is produced on female plants. Male plants have small yellow flowers in spring, dispensing clouds of golden pollen.

Yew forms a dense, solid hedge and is ideal for topiary. Old hedges and trees may be drastically pruned, throwing new growths the following year. Yew wood is highly prized by craftsmen and ranges in colour from cream through fawn to deep brown and pink.

Yew will not survive if planted in waterlogged ground. It tolerates acid or alkaline soil and prefers a deep, moist, fertile, well-drained site in full sun or partial shade. It will grow quite quickly to a height of 15m (50ft) with a spread of 10m (33ft).

left

TAXUS BACCATA
A beautiful timber for furniture, it won't knot in a thousand years.

below

TAXUS BACCATA 'STANDISHII'
A female form of golden English yew with red arils.

Taxus baccata 'Fastigiata'

IRISH YEW, FLORENCECOURT YEW

In 1779 two seedling yews were found growing with heather on a hillside in County Fermanagh, Northern Ireland. The farmer, Mr Willis, dug them up, replanted one in his garden and gave the second to his landlord, the Earl of Enniskillen, who planted it at Florencecourt. From this source tens of millions of one of the great yews have been grown.

As a young plant it forms a narrow, compact column of tightly packed branches. Eventually it becomes broader at the top. The evergreen leaves are black-green on the upper surface, dull green on the underside. It is a female plant with bright red fruit or arils that stand out against the almost black foliage. The green seed first forms a cap similar to that of an acorn. The cap swells around the

above

TAXUS BACCATA 'SUMMERGOLD'
Given the space, this yew will cover a lot of ground; its evergreen foliage smothering most weeds.

left

TAXUS BACCATA 'FASTIGIATA'
A wonderful upright fastigiate conifer which, in the fullness of time, will spread to 7m (23ft).

seed, leaving an opening at the tip, and becomes the red outer flesh. The seed is highly poisonous.

Irish yew will tolerate most soil conditions with the exception of waterlogged ground. It prefers a moist, fertile, well-drained soil. A moist climate is preferred (the average annual rainfall in County Fermanagh is 170cm/68in).

Plant in full sun or partial shade. Deep shade will encourage the top to spread and become shaggy, but it can be clipped annually. In areas of heavy snow the upright branches may need to be tied-in to avoid the weight of snow spoiling the shape. It will grow to a height of 13m (43ft) with a spread of 7m (23ft).

Taxus baccata 'Fastigiata Aureomarginata'

GOLDEN IRISH YEW

The only thing wrong with this plant is its sex. It is male and doesn't have the benefit of berries. Slower-growing than 'Fastigiata', it makes a superb conifer, remaining small for many years. It can be planted either as a single specimen or as a line, to form columns of gold. The leaves are edged with bright golden yellow. In the second year the gold fades to light green.

It will grow well in acid or alkaline soil, providing it is not waterlogged. Biting cold winds or strong sun may scorch the foliage of young plants. It will grow to a height of 6m (20ft) with a spread of 3m (10ft).

Taxus baccata 'Summergold'

This yew forms a low shrubby plant with upward spreading branches. It is excellent for ground cover, smothering out all but the most persistent weeds. The evergreen leaves are bright golden yellow in summer, turning to dark green with a yellow margin in winter.

It is not particular regarding soil, even thriving on impoverished ground, providing it is not waterlogged. Plant it in a lightly shaded site as strong, direct sun will scorch the foliage.

It will grow to a height of 75cm (30in) with a spread of 8m (26ft).

There are many other excellent varieties of *T. baccata* including 'Lutea', which was a chance discovery in 1817 in Dublin by a Mr Whitlaw. I mention it because it is female and displays masses of bright yellow berries which look fantastic against the dark green leaves. It grows to a height of 4m (13ft) with a similar spread.

Thuja occidentalis

WHITE CEDAR, EASTERN CEDAR, ARBOR VITAE

What's in a name? *Thuja* is sometimes incorrectly written as *thuya*, which is how it is pronounced. *Thuja* is Greek for 'unknown species'. In France, *arbor vitae*, Latin for 'tree of life', was used to describe it in the eighteenth century. *Occidentalis* means 'of the west' and the tree is native to America, so that at least is correct. Why then, do Americans call it the eastern cedar? It's not even a cedar.

Call it what you will, it is a beautiful, medium-sized, evergreen, columnar tree with orange-brown peeling bark. The yellowish green, scale-like leaves are pale green on the underside, turning bronze-green in winter. When crushed they give off a fragrance of apple. The leaves form flattened sprays along the spreading branches. The 1cm (0.5in) long, female cones are green and smooth.

above

THUJA OCCIDENTALIS
Whatever you choose to call it, it has lovely foliage and eye-catching bark.

It prefers a deep, moist, well-drained, fertile soil. As it dislikes transplanting, purchase it as a small plant. Grow it in full sun and, until it is established, protect it from cold winds. It will grow to a height of 20m (66ft) with a spread of 4m (13ft).

Thuja occidentalis 'Rheingold'

A beautiful conifer which often causes confusion and arguments because it produces both juvenile and adult foliage. Plants sold with juvenile growths will remain dwarf and rounded and the foliage will be feathery. Plants propagated from growths with adult foliage will quickly form a tall columnar conifer with adult foliage. The leaf colour of both plants will be golden-yellow in summer, turning to a superb coppery-bronze shade in winter.

It dislikes a waterlogged soil. For good winter colour plant this conifer in an open site without shade. As a dot plant in a bed of winter-flowering heathers it has few equals.

It will grow to a height of 4m (13ft) with a spread of 3m (10ft).

Thuja orientalis 'Aurea Nana'

'Aurea Nana' forms a dense, globular, bushy plant with fern-like foliage. The leaves are bright butter-yellow in summer turning a paler yellowish green in winter. In severe weather or exposed sites it may become bronzy-yellow in winter.

'Aurea nana' makes an ideal choice for a low ornamental hedge. A light clipping in late spring will encourage it to give a good show.

It prefers a moist, fertile, well-drained soil. Plant in full sun or light shade. It will grow to a height of 1.6m (5ft) with a spread of 1m (3ft).

Thuja plicata 'Atrovirens'
WESTERN RED CEDAR

I love this adaptable conifer. It is superior to leyland cypress (x *Cuprocyparis leylandii*) as a tall screen. As a tight, evergreen hedge it will give yew a run for its money.

It is not a cedar but the foliage, when crushed, has a wonderful aromatic smell. I have planted and maintain a maze of 'Atrovirens' and after a day's clipping I smell great. At least I think so.

It is fast-growing, forming a pyramidal plant with red-brown bark. The leaves are glossy, dark green with paler green undersides marked with white-grey. Even old plants may be cut hard, regrowing with fresh foliage within one year. It is happy to be transplanted as a large specimen, providing care is taken to prevent foliage and roots drying out during the first growing season.

It can tolerate heavy, wet ground but prefers a deep, moist, fertile soil. Plant it in full sun with shelter from cold winds. It will grow to a height of 15m (50ft) with a spread of 5m (16ft).

above left
THUJA PLICATA 'ATROVIRENS'
Apart from disliking cold winds this is a most adaptable tree, putting up with hard pruning, transplanting and heavy, wet soil.

above
TSUGA CANADENSIS 'PENDULA'
When it comes to covering ground, this conifer has better spreading qualities than paint.

Tsuga canadensis 'Pendula'
EASTERN HEMLOCK

If you want to cover a wall or steep bank from above then this is an ideal plant. It will not do it overnight but it will do it well. On the other hand, when trained with a clear stem, it makes a superb evergreen weeping conifer for planting as a specimen on a lawn.

Its normal habit is prostrate, covering everything in its path as it spreads, although the overlapping branches, over time, build up to form a dumpy, spreading bush. Planted beside a vertical drop, it cascades down with bright, mid-green, soft foliage.

It prefers a moist, well-drained, fertile, acid soil, although it will tolerate a little lime. It dislikes a cold wind, which may brown the foliage.

When trained as a standard weeping tree it will always need to be supported with a stake. Left to spread, it will grow to 2m (6ft 6in) with a spread of 8m (26ft).

Tsuga heterophylla
WESTERN HEMLOCK

This makes an excellent hedge or, if you have a large lawn of about 1 hectare (2½ acres) there is no nicer conifer to plant. It will form a narrow, conical tree with red-brown bark and horizontal branches that droop at the tips. The evergreen leaves are glossy dark green with white bands on the underside, double-ranked on grey stems.

It prefers an acid to neutral, moist, well-drained, fertile soil. Plant it in a site sheltered from cold winds in sun or shade. When grown as a hedge, clip in early summer to allow regrowth before winter. As a specimen tree, it will grow to a massive height of 30-40m (100-130ft) with a spread of 10m (33ft).

INDEX

ACKNOWLEDGEMENTS

With grateful thanks to Caroline Taggart for her patience, common sense and professionalism.

The publishers and photographers would like to thank Ray Broughton, Mark Ekin and the staff and students of Sparsholt College, Hampshire, for their assistance with the step-by-step photography; Hamish Cathie, for his patience in allowing repeated visits to his garden; Colin Morgan at Bedgebury National Pinetum, Simon Toomer at Westonbirt Arboretum, and Hilliers Arboretum for their generosity and expertise; Magda Haire at Handcross Park for help with *Prunus* photographs; and the Brogdale Trust for *Malus*.

Key: HA = Heather Angel; GPL = Garden Picture Library; Holt = Holt Studios International Ltd; DB = Deni Bown; AL = Andrew Lawson; t = top; b = bottom; l = left; r = right

All photography by Sarah Cuttle except:

Step-by-step photography on pages 76-91 by Christopher Cormack

page 3 HA; 14 GPL/Didier Willery; 16 Holt/Rosemary Mayer; 20/21 HA; 21 GPL/John Glover; 23 DB; 24 Holt/Bob Gibbons; 25 DB; 26 HA; 26/27 GPL /John Glover; 27 Holt/Bob Gibbons; 28 Holt/Bob Gibbons; 28/29 John Cushnie; 29 GPL/Howard Rice; 30 Holt/ Gordon Roberts; 30/31 GPL/Ron Evans; 31 GPL/Howard Rice; 34 Holt/Peter WIlson; 35(l) Holt/Bob Gibbons; 35(r) GPL/John Glover; 36 HA; 36-37 Holt/Bob Gibbons; 37, 38 DB; 40 GPL/John Glover; 41(l) GPL/Didier Willery; 41(r) Holt/Bob Gibbons; 42/43 AL; 43 DB; 44 Holt/Primrose Peacock; 44-45 GPL/Steven Wooster; 45 GPL/Howard Rice; 47(r), 49, 50 HA; 50/51 GPL/Juliette Wade; 51 HA; 52 Holt/Peter Wilson; 53 Holt/Primrose Peacock; 54/55 HA; 56 DB; 57 GPL/Howard Rice; 60(l) GPL/Brigitte Thomas; 60(r) GPL/Howard Rice; 61 GPL/John Glover; 74-75 HA; 77 GPL/Heik Dijkman; 83(t) HA; 86 Holt/Nigel Cattlin; 92(l) Holt; 92(r) Holt/Nigel Cattlin; 93(t) Holt/Nigel Cattlin; 93(b) GPL/Lamontagne; 94 Holt/Nigel Cattlin; 95(t & br) Holt/Nigel Cattlin; 95(bl) HA; 96(t) Holt/Willem Harinck; 96(b) Holt/Nigel Cattllin; 97(t) HA; 97 (bl, bm) Holt/Nigel Cattlin; 97 (br) Holt/Duncan Smith; 98 Steven Wooster; 101 GPL/Howard Rice; 102-3 HA; 105 AL; 106, 107, 108, 110 HA; 111 AL; 130-1, 132 HA; 139(r) GPL/John Miller; 140-141 GPL/DavidEngland; 143(l) Red Cover/Hugh Palmer; 143(r), 144(t) DB; 144(b); 145 AL; 146-7 GPL/Clive Boursnell; 148, 149(t) HA; 151 GPL/ Howard Rice; 154-5 GPL/J S Sira; 155 Global Book Publishing; 159 AL; 161(r) DB;162 GPL/Mark Bolton; 163 HA; 164-5 DB; 170 HA; 172 AL; 174 GPL/John Glover; 175 AL; 176 Holt/ Rosemary Mayer; 177 GPL/Didier Willery; 185(t), 187(b) DB; 188 GPL/Neil Holmes; 191 GPL/John Ferro Sims; 192-3 HA; 193(r) GPL/J S Sira; 194 GPL/David Askham;194-5 GPL/Mark Bolton; 195 GPL/Brigittte Thomas; 208 HA; 215(t) GPL/John Glover; 215(b) GPL/David Russell; 216(l) Holt/Bob Gibbons; 219(r) GPL/Lamontagne